Quest for Presence:
Experience and Praise

Joel Bennett is a true 'connoisseur of time.' His *Quest for Presence* helps in savoring one's own life story in chaos and in flow and everything in between. If you take the time to learn it, you'll have more patience when conditions are not nurturing and thus more of your time becomes effortless, momentous, and poignant. The *Quest for Presence* helps the ordinary become resonant.

—Stephen Kiesling, Editor in Chief, *Spirituality + Health* magazine; Member, USA Olympic Rowing Team (1980)

The *Quest for Presence* work brings out the wisdom of the ages to become the magic of the moment. And this requires going inward. Here is an analogy that best describes this shift. Washing the glass patio door, I faced the common dilemma of determining on which side the dirt resides. After reviewing the inside, my hunch was that the grime was outside. It makes sense because most of the soot comes from outside. So, I clean outside as thoroughly as I can. I walk back into the house and realize the dirt really was on the inside all along. Go inside. Join the *Quest for Presence*.

—Alan Porzio, Sound Designer, Third Ear Sound Design

As we seek to understand our life experiences and the world around us, it helps to have a guide—a trusted source that can help decipher life's meaning and make sense of our short time on earth. That guide can be a leader, a loved one, a mentor, or even a scribe. Dr. Bennett has a magical way of shape-shifting all these roles to shepherd you on your wisdom quest. He leads you on a journey of self-exploration and deep reflection in an easy-to-consume process. Dr. Bennett's insights and wisdom have deeply impacted my life. I am delighted that he is now sharing this gift with everyone. Get ready to embark on your transformation. You will learn a new way of being—both in time and beyond time.

—Ryan Picarella, MS, Chief Executive Officer,
Wellness Councils of America

The *Quest for Presence* has been a valuable exploration for me to discover more about the truth of who I am, and for discovering my relationship to time. From the initial invitation to 'listen' in the introductory *The Connoisseur of Time: An Invitation to Presence,* two statements deeply resonated with me and have been touchstones for forward movement on my own quest. They are 'I am aware of and attracted to timeless and eternal qualities; my truest identity is ultimately beyond time' and 'My day is filled with treasures, day-to-day, every day.'

The live interactive sessions in the *Quest for Presence* series are treasure-full opportunities to 'speak aloud' my awareness cultivated through the materials, and share in community. The author has a gift for taking deep, meaningful, and contemplative information and translating it in inviting, thought-provoking and fun ways that ignite and cultivate awareness and a sense of coming home. I highly recommend all humans to consider going on this amazing, fun, inspiring, and uplifting journey of self-discovery and self-care.

—Kimberly Gray, RN, Integrative Health and Wellness Consultant;
HeartMath Master Trainer/Coach/Mentor

Quest for Presence is Dr. Joel Bennett's gift and invitation to meander around the Map of Radiant Forces; to reimagine our unique understanding of time while catching glimpses of our collective, woven humanity. Each chapter offers opportunities to contemplate the material through one or more questions that ask us to PAUSE. Dr. Bennett allows us to become vulnerable with ourselves as he reflects candidly.

As I navigate the Map of a new perspective of time, I ask myself how to answer the question 'How are you holding it together?' I can laugh or cry over this, and my answer can change at any moment. In his wisdom though, Dr. Bennett asks 'WHAT IF, AT SOME DEEPEST AND MOST TRUE LEVEL, WE ARE ALL BEING HELD TOGETHER?'

Indeed! Together. A loving community of explorers, open to all who are curious. We are called to be Time Weavers. We intersect, share, and support each other. I hope you'll join us. Collect the many Treasures on this journey. Explore this Gift, and as a result you will remember even more treasures await.

—Becky Papa, MEd, Reiki Master; Photographer

I love this work and the 'totality' of it all. It has given me a new perspective of letting go of the things, memories, occasions that do not fulfill my soul, and embrace the beauty and simplicity of presence. There is joy in the simplicity of the ordinary—it is bringing me a new-found freedom as I gain a deeper understanding of how my personality attracts the Radiant Forces and how the Attractions feed the deepest depths of my soul to weave and flow from one force to another.

Every time I open the book or listen to a podcast or participate in the workshops with other time weavers, I learn something new to guide me through my *quest for presence*. The Soulful Capacities give me the ability to deconstruct the parts of my life that do not serve my soul and reconstruct them into a new path that brings growth and prosperity. The path never ends, it continually changes as it winds through different forces that influence my presence in the moment.

Life is a precious gift. How I choose to utilize the gift in its entirety is completely up to me. I practice daily to be present, aware, and open to seeking the beauty of what was, what is, what will be. Finding the treasures within each one of those moments is a gift that feeds my soul. 'Our souls know what our personalities only dimly perceive.' The gift of the *Quest for Presence* has changed my life. The impact has been nothing short of amazing.

—Amanda Jo Edelmayer, Culture Development Lead,
Battelle Energy Alliance

Reading and discussing *Quest for Presence* with others on the journey has been both intellectually stimulating and intensely practical. The idea of time as a tapestry, a precious weave rather than a straight line, immediately resonated with me. Joel takes this idea and shows its many implications. In one of our discussions, each of us had the opportunity to share an application from the book. Mine was the idea to 'not take any of it too seriously except for a regular and dedicated practice that enhances your spirit....' For me this has been morning and evening meditation and prayer. Of course, as a serious-minded person, I took to heart the one thing Joel said I should be serious about, and it has really made a difference in my life!

—Ben Dilla, PhD, Director, Doctor of Business Administration
(DBA) Program, University of Dallas

As I progressed through the reading of *Quest for Presence*, I began to feel overwhelmed with terms and concepts. As I continued to apply the concepts to my life, my biography in particular, something other than overwhelm arose. Instead of experiencing the words and concepts in a linear format, like something to memorize—I began to feel the layered experience of them and the movement within my life! Suddenly, instead of feeling like I had some things to memorize and understand, my experiences began to give rise to an understanding of some of the words and concepts. I became more alive to my life, seeing the reflection in the maps that I was learning.

This quote from the book had meaning for me: 'Life is happening. The process of this happening life may be complex but finding purpose and joy within it need not be complicated.' I could see that merely being present to learning AND experiencing is not complicated but a refreshing way to BE with my life as it unfolds. And having words that reflect forces of the universe in my experience of this happening life enlivens my soul.

—Michele Mariscal, PhD, Owner, EnergyM

Quest for Presence. The title itself, I find inviting: the invitation to participate in our own life party, one that is fascinating, with lots of friends, family, and perhaps new acquaintances, all in our beautiful universe. All you have to do is first show up with your heart and mind, so much there to explore and so much treasure to be had. Through this series of books, my friend and author Dr. Joel Bennett is guiding me with the map in my own life journey to explore. He is telling us to participate in not just clock time but learn to participate in deeper time. He has so many enlightening wisdom quotes in the book. Most of them send a deep message that it is not about your time and my time. In truth, we all belong together in time; with Radiant Forces within us, we have infinite time. Let us all show up to our life journey and explore our treasures.

—Dr. Dazzle B. Shrestha, DC, Chiropractor, Eastside Chiropractic

Dr. Bennett's *Quest for Presence* books and workshops weave together the threads of time, philosophy, and personal growth to offer a transformative experience for those ready to receive. Dr. Bennett guides you through a journey of personal stories, insightful quotes, and contemplative exercises to help you build a more meaningful relationship with time and wellbeing. But the book is only the beginning. The true value, for me, is meeting the people who participate in the workshops. Dr.

Bennett has a gift for attracting the most interesting— and diverse— participants. We always seem to start the workshop as strangers and end the workshop as companions on the journey.

—Michele Studer, MBA, Organizational Change, Change Management and Services Process Manager, Fujitsu Network Communications

The writer of the *Book of Ecclesiastes* reminds us 'for everything there is a season, and a time to every purpose under heaven.' Given that we are now living in a season of perpetual volatility, uncertainty, complexity, and ambiguity, it is my belief that Dr. Joel Bennett's *Quest for Presence* Workshop was divinely inspired for 'such a time as this.'

Dr. Bennett's work has dramatically improved the quality of my life. Throughout the Workshop, I was guided on how to pause (to quest, to go within), to become fully present with and learning to listen to myself and others intimately.

I received practical yet powerful insight, knowledge, tools, and resources that enabled me to make immediate, positive, and permanent adjustments to my attitudes and actions.

As a baby-boomer and trauma survivor, many of my experiences, challenges, and accomplishments can be linked to workaholism and other unhealthy coping behaviors. Intentionally taking time to pause, rest, refresh, relax, meditate, reflect, and be fully present has rarely, if ever, been something that I valued or practiced. Occasional brief interludes of quietness or stillness have always felt uncomfortable, seemed unnatural and totally counter-productive—I viewed these things as the ultimate waste of valuable time.

That errant perception changed, and a new season, time, and purpose began for me when I embarked on a life-changing *quest for presence* adventure, as facilitated by Dr. Bennett.

—Cheryl Brown Merriwether, MSHRDA, SHRM-SCP, SPHR, CM, CRSS, CPRC, Vice President/Executive Director: ICARE (International Center for Addiction and Recovery Education)

There are so many reflections and insights that were, and still are, sparked by this work. I use the tool of recognizing presence to recover or reclaim my strength and resilience. This is particularly key when those dark, hidden moments pop up to trigger my most basic instincts. Reflecting instead of resisting helps me to better manage or release that energy. I am grateful for the light that follows.

—Janet Fouts, Founder and Coach, Nearly Mindful

Quest for Presence has had a profound impact on my life. As someone who loves my work, it is easy to tip into 'too busy' and a sense of being time poor. I read this book with the goal of learning to be more present. WOW. It showed me the bigger picture 'map' of Forces that affect time, and it was like someone dropped a YOU ARE HERE pin on that map. The book and workshop helped me to realize I already have a lot of presence-building traits that I can leverage, and gave me important tools to help me 'drop into' presence, which I now use daily. As a result, I feel more at peace, more trusting, less anxious, and more in charge of my own life. It has been truly transformative – and I am excited to read the next installment.

—Melanie White, Co-Founder; Sage Women's Health

Quest
for
PRESENCE

BOOK 2

THE SOULFUL CAPACITIES

Joel B. Bennett, PhD

ORGANIZATIONAL WELLNESS AND LEARNING SYSTEMS

QUEST FOR PRESENCE MANDALA

The Radiant Forces

Form

Chaos

Nurturing
Conditions

Time
Shaping

The Soulful Capacities

Acceptance

Presence

Flow

Synchronicity

The Attractions

Crafting

Potentiating

Discerning

Centering

Synthesizing

Coordinating

Intending

Catalyzing

Opening

The Trajectories

Transcendence —   — Interruption

Rhythm —   — Pacing

Timing —   — Routine

Transition —   — Scheduling

The Treasures

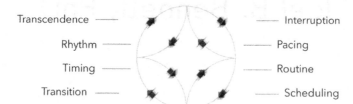

Start here and
flow clockwise

← Spontaneity → Momentousness → Fulfillment → Clutch →
Optimism → Effortlessness → Ordinariness → Coherence →
Adoration → Resonance → Patience → Preciousness →
Savoring → Poignance → Release → Awe → Spontaneity →

Published by

Organizational Wellness and Learning Systems

FLOWER MOUND, TX

ISBN-13: 978-0-9915102-4-5 (Paperback)
          978-0-9915102-5-2 (Ebook)
          978-0-9915102-8-3 (Hardback)

Editing by Candace Johnson, Change It Up Editing, Inc.; and
Sue Hansen, Duck Sauce Life, Inc.

Cover and interior by Gary A. Rosenberg

Mandala art by author, Jeffrey McQuirk, and Rob Supan.

Back cover art, "Whirling Dervish" by Spencer Seidman

*At that very moment when one realizes
the glory of the witness, the soul,
one begins to enjoy transcendence
beyond the time of material energy;*

*One becomes immediately free from
misconceptions of "I" and "mine,"
and manifests as Pure Consciousness.*

~ŚRĪMAD BHĀGAVATAM
(CANTO 2, CHAPTER 9, VERSE 3)

Quest for Presence Collection

. . . and for the unfolding of the greater plan,
this life, your destiny . . .

Contents

Foreword

I have known Joel Bennett for over 40 years. When we first met, he was a man on a quest! His intention was evident. His questions indicated he longed to find the truths of Nature, both the way of things and human nature. His good humor and sharp mind let me know he would find something original, unique, and universal. It is said that those who seek will find; in Joel's case, he came upon the treasures of an awakened mind and heart, seeking to know expression as an active presence in our lives.

Welcome to his new work, *Quest for Presence: The Soulful Capacities*. When asked to explain QfP, he described certain qualities necessary for the quest: Acceptance, Presence, Flow, and Synchronicity. My life work has been understanding and teaching how spiritual astrology relates to humanistic psychology. As you may know, true astrology is about discerning, navigating, and embracing one's unique destiny. So, these four qualities immediately piqued my curiosity. I see these as qualities to be cultivated as we embrace a conscious, Soul-centered life. And I believe this book, with its many exercises, contemplations, stories, poems, and research, will guide you in your journey.

I believe that the Soul is the Love we aspire to and the Love we are. This Love is inextricably united with the One Love we all are together. The Soul is always both seeking and finding its own expression. Each Soulful Capacity allows us to glimpse, feel, and even bathe in this expression.

Acceptance

Acceptance is a key for all who want Love to manifest in the world. When we accept ourselves as we are in each moment of life, our challenges become opportunities to develop a Soulful response. Our Soul seeks expression. Life brings countless opportunities for that expression—especially as we accept the task of shaping our personality so that our Higher Self can express the Loving Wise Intelligence of our Soul.

We discover a transcendent power when we accept that we grow more from pain, loss, and challenges than from comfort. We are Eternals having human experiences. Our Soul expresses more fully when we embrace challenges as opportunities. As a work in progress, we find power as we open to the mystery path of our self-unfoldment. There is beauty and comfort knowing that we share that path with millions across time—where we each find our unique purpose for being alive.

Presence

Presence involves being here and now. Many people spend time wishing they were somewhere else or doing something else. They rarely experience *what* they are doing and *where* they are doing it. Clock-time's constant pressures and decisions distract them from the precious moment.

When I choose to remember now is the only time there is, I automatically experience Presence. I have learned that nothing outside matters as much as my response to it. When I am fully present in the moment, external things pass through my mind and life while I stay centered and focused on what matters.

I have discovered a secret to happiness: It is far more satisfying to identify with what is within and permanent than with externals that fade away. Presence calls forth compassion, gratitude, and appreciation. When I generate these expressions, they are strengthened in the collective field with others and in my environment.

Flow

Flow allows for the perfection of a series of moments. We know there is no other unfolding than now. Flow allows us to detach from hopes, fears, or immediately pressing issues. Flow is Presence-in-motion, whether moving and acting, or contemplating which direction to steer the Flow.

Flow liberates us to surrender to life's rhythms. We are precisely *where* we need to be *when* we need to be there—whether we are doing *what* needs to be done or simply "being" *who* we need to be. Flow helps us greet each moment as pure potential—whether to say goodbye or hello. We respond in new ways rather than stay stuck in unworkable ideas.

Synchronicity

Synchronicity is being in harmony with the truth and magic of the moment. All that is *meant to be* arises at that moment. Through Synchronicity, we find that all that is "true" can be facilitated, while all that is "not true" is frustrating. Synchronicity is the moment-to-moment freshness—a point in space and time with a unique potentiality for us to "do our being."

Through the magical coincidence of Synchronicity, we realize we are our "answer to the need of that moment." All things occur at designated times which help us choose specific responses. When we know that everything is happening as planned, we deepen awareness, growing and developing as we should at each turn of life's wheel.

Adventure Through the Timestream of Life

The Soulful Capacities are ever present in the Timestream of Life. They are innate qualities, but our personalities learn habits that block our soulfulness. As children, we learn to be more comfortable with the devil we know than the heaven we do not. We are brainwashed into clock-time while deep time keeps dancing with our souls in the background.

Each of us is called every moment to remember the dance. Our personality learned many things which obscure our eternal Self. We learned to clutch at "good feelings," avoid "bad feelings," and "think the right things." And yet we know we are Souls, beyond anything we think or feel.

The Soulful Capacities come with many benefits. We grow to accept our destiny. We realize the Presence of our Eternal Self. We naturally flow with life because we are not hung up on fear, hope, anticipation, or resistance. And Synchronicity awakens us to the greater mystery of our life in this cosmos. Ultimately, we have a higher Destiny, which is called Dharma, or Tao in the East. Our Dharma is to be lived, and will be lived, regardless of what we believe. Flowing with the Tao, we face and quickly dispel our fear.

The Soulful Capacities have broad application across many healing and spiritual arts. As an astrologer, I study destiny through the birth chart—a map of the sky (stars, planets) at the time, date, and location of one's birth on planet Earth. This chart shows the pure potentiality of our soul's expression across the twelve zodiac signs and twelve frequency zones of human existence. These zones are the material, emotional, mental, and spiritual levels of three dimensions of experience: personal, interpersonal, and transpersonal.

Our birth chart reveals innate tendencies we are called to cultivate, transmuting dysfunction into healthy Soulful responses. Our chart also shows us "to everything there is a season." Essentially, there are times when we must make life-altering choices, embracing the adventure of our potential while leaving behind unfulfilling actions, thoughts, and feelings.

Meant to Be

The message of Quest for Presence is clear. It encourages us to embark on this adventure at any time we want, cultivating our potential and aligning with our Soul to express our personality's finest qualities. Become one with the corrective force of Nature Herself. These activities will bring The Love We Are into synchronistic contact with other loving, wise intelligences.

Destiny gives birth to these contacts. They were meant to be, just as I am sure you will come to greater awareness by what you find (contact) in this book. The great truth is that we are all more capable together than we are separate.

No matter what your spiritual beliefs may be, this powerful work provides the tools to remember your Soul and its qualities. As you transcend linear clock-time, you will live in the joy of self-discovery, and will find peace and power in identifying with that part of you which eternally loves, seeks understanding, and finds wisdom in perfection, truth, purpose, and fulfillment.

Welcome to your destiny.

Robert Wilkinson
Publisher: Aquariuspapers.com
Author:
Love Dad: Healing the Grief of Losing a Stillborn (2002)
A New Look at Mercury Retrograde (2014)
Saturn: Spiritual Master, Spiritual Friend (2016)
The Magic of Venus: Friendships, Soul Mates, and Twin Flames (2022)
The Cycles of Life: The 7 Year Cycles (in production)

Author Note

Quest for Presence, or QfP for short, includes five books. Each can be read independently or as part of the whole; they need not be read in sequence. If you are just entering the collection, welcome! Your journey begins with QfP Book 2: *The Soulful Capacities*.

QfP is written and structured to support your sense that the particular book you are reading is just right for you. Indeed, the notion of time in QfP is about being wherever you happen to be.

Readers of QfP like that it has a "choose your own adventure" quality, offering a variety of entry points for engaging with core concepts. If you are new to these topics, I recommend that you read straight through each book. Please pause to review the contemplations at the end of most chapters (or complete corresponding activities in the QfP *Contemplations Workbook*, or both). It will help to read my personal reflections, as they illustrate how these concepts render in real life.

Each book also comes with notes in a research notes section, many of which relate to the science of time or provide references for readers interested in the related concept in the text. QfP is informed by a vast literature in the growing study and philosophy of time. However, these books are not intended to be evidence-based or academic. I am not summoning research to advance a new science of presence. I hope you will explore these notes only when your curiosity outweighs your desire to achieve time competency.

By time competency, I mean the ability to return to living in the present moment of your whole life (staying "on script," as it were).

There are two steps to being time competent. First, you notice when anxiety, worry, longing, or overthinking (your mental future) pull you away from the adventure; or when regret, remorse, self-judgment, or ruminations (your mental past) push you out of the moment. Second, you gently return to the here and now and the feeling that your whole-time is a happening, unfolding, or awesome life journey.

If you are re-entering the collection by way of another starting point, I invite you to reconnect to your journey. As is the nature of any quest, wherever you are along your path—and whichever book you find yourself reading—there you are.

The title of this book changed often as it went into final edits. This dynamic is a contemplation in itself. Does the way a book appears—judging a book by its title—make any difference to how you arrived here? I have listed the titles below. I think they all work. But the world requires us to fix things into a lasting word or image. I hope you find one that resonates with you.

A Quest for Presence, This Happening Life, Time's Precious Weave, Your Journey of Wholeness, Finding Free Time This Whole Time, Recovering Time in a World Addicted to Distraction and *Contemplations for Your Whole Time Here.*

* * *

I encourage you to download a free copy of the preview to *QfP* on our website www.presencequest.life. *The Connoisseur of Time: An Invitation to Presence* has helped many get a solid grasp of the reason for this journey. You will also find resources and events on our site to support you in your quest.

About the Abbreviation Q*f*P

The *f* symbol between Q and P (a letter f with a descender hook) is the notation used in mathematics to represent functions. Specifically, functions represent how a varying quantity depends on another quantity. For example, the position of a planet is a function of time, or a weekly salary is a function of the hourly pay rate and the number of hours worked, or supply is a function of demand: As price goes up, demand goes down. In our quest for presence, our journey is a function of our presence, and at the same time, our presence is a function of our journey. As you become more present, the experience of life as a happening adventure and unfoldment is more enhanced. As your experience of life enhances, you become more present. The thrill is in the ride, and the ride is in the thrill.

Introduction to All Books

To be present means to be present to the whole time of your life. Being here now is important. Equally important is your whole life—where you came from and where you are headed. We just don't live in the now. Our whole life is a project of purpose and meaning, a coming into being, a path of sense-making, a place where everything fits together, a journey, a becoming, an arrival, a fulfillment of destiny, a momentous emergence, a cause, a calling, an awakening, and so much more. And all of these occur outside of "clock-time."

Presence happens when we show up and fully engage in this life with all its changes, interruptions, and distractions. Our presence is imperfect. This collection of books encourages you to embrace its imperfections. Our attention faces many challenges: advertisements, attention deficit, abuse, anxiety, aging, and cognitive decline, to name a few. Life is fleeting, a blur. How can you find the time to live it and live it well? Perhaps it's time to embrace the blur of your whole-time here.

This Quest for Presence (QfP) collection is designed to help you reach any number of objectives. This includes the actual letting go of specific deadlines in favor of contemplations that improve your presence. This idea may seem radical in a society oriented toward action, achievement, and accomplishment. As you will discover, this orientation is born out of a narrow-minded, fragmenting, and dys-functional view that time comprises only "clock-time." A different, contemplative objective would be that you stop long enough to enjoy the rich, full, and precious aspects of this very brief life.

The Q*f*P is about making room for uplifts, for positive moments, for glimpses of the amazing wonders and emotions that life has to offer. I call these *Treasures*. My hope is that you will become more inquisitive about these Treasures. Where do they come from? How can you experience them more frequently? Are you prone to experiencing certain kinds more than others? Through the Q*f*P, I believe you will get answers to these questions. Your view of time will change. You will have more well-being, wholeness, and intimacy in your life—both with others and with the ever-evolving natural world.

Other objectives stem from these questions. A new perspective may help you be more efficient. To value your time in a new way may give you the motivation and tools to prioritize what matters most. Alternatively, as you discover the big picture of time—as delineated here—you may grow in your sense of spirituality, faith, and transcendence of life's problems. My personal aim for you lies in between these two areas: efficiency and spirituality. This happens by embracing the ordinariness of life by becoming present to it.

Whatever your troubles, a shared presence can also make you resilient and thrive. This quest for presence is meant to be shared. We have arrived here as conscious beings because of cosmic forces that modern physics has only begun to understand. Deterioration of intimacy is the greatest problem of time compression (see my book *Time and Intimacy: A New Science of Personal Relationships* [Erlbaum, 2000]). We cannot appreciate our time without each other. As such, this offering is also a memoir. I hope you get to know me well enough so you feel less alone and more connected. And since we are here, we might as well make the most of it. Together.

Introduction to Book 2:
The Soulful Capacities

The human soul connects heaven—the eternal—and earth—the temporary or temporal—and embodies deeper forces (the four Cosmic Radiant Forces: Time Shaping, Form, Nurturing Conditions, and Chaos), which are explored in *QfP Book 1*. Our essence, a synonym for the soul, matures and flourishes through our quest. This book helps you identify and develop four capacities that allow you to get in touch with your essence. Through these capacities, you bring your unique gifts into the world.

This book is divided into three parts. Part One prepares you for study. Part Two dives into each of the Soulful Capacities. These are Acceptance, Presence, Flow, and Synchronicity. Part Three offers Contemplations, the Temple, the Veil, and Preciousness.

In Part One, chapter 1 prepares you for study of the Soulful Capacities, and chapter 2 reviews some key definitions that may help you understand them better. You can read these preparations or dive right into each of the Soulful Capacities in Part Two: Acceptance (chapter 3), Presence (chapter 4), Flow (chapter 5), and Synchronicity (chapter 6). For each, I offer an introduction, exercises, discussion questions, relevant quotations, and a self-assessment. These self-assessments, along with your personality assessment in *QfP Book 3* (the Attractions), give you a comprehensive picture of how your essence and personality dance together on your quest for presence.

Part Three begins with a call to reflect on the divine origin of the soul. Chapter 7 came to me as an intercession. One day I woke up feeling that a force (an intuitive jolt) intervened to make sure I wrote chapter 7. As part of cultivating any of the four capacities, we learn to contemplate (chapter 8) and understand spiritual health and self-transcendence (chapter 9). Through Contemplation, we see that our life—our temporary human body—can be treated like a Temple, and our physical senses capture only a thin layer of the total experience available to us. As we do, we gain a keener awareness of the Veil of the material world (chapter 10). Finally, all of this heightens our appreciation of the Preciousness of life, the opportunity given through human birth (chapter 11).

The final chapter (12) helps readers synthesize exercises in previous chapters. Accordingly, you can integrate the self-assessments in chapters 3 through 6 into a final overall assessment of your own Soulful Capacity to experience and befriend time as a life-giving resource. The next book in QfP (Book 3) also contains assessments. Combined with the results in chapter 12, these assessments make up the *Quest for Presence Inventory*™ (QFPI™). The two assessments (of Soulful Capacities here in Book 2 and of Attractions in Book 3) stand independently of each other. Please explore either alone or together in your own time and as your journey unfolds.

A note to readers who completed Book 1 of the QfP collection. In Book 1, I describe the Time Adjustment Protocol as a way to understand and let go of worry, anxiety, rumination, and the need to control. Our difficulty with these negative states is exacerbated by clock-time and the pressures of living in a time-imprisoning culture. Book 1 showed that the roots of these mental problems can be traced to processes that transcend all culture: the neutral, objective, and ever unfolding Radiant Forces. Much of modern psychology attempts to analyze and even uproot these problems. In contrast, QfP encourages you to see everything as workable. Nothing to analyze. Nothing to uproot. In Book 1, you learned where these concerns come from. Here, in Book 2, you will learn—through Acceptance, Presence, Flow, and Synchronicity—how to carefully trace these roots to their source and uncover many treasures along the way.

Book 1 also described the Radiant Forces as a *totality that holds us* and from which everything *unfolds* in and through time. As we let go of clock-time, we learn acceptance from surrendering to the totality, cultivate presence by allowing our lives to be held, and experience flow as the unfolding of our lives. Meaning, purpose, and the treasures of life—all aspects of synchronicity—come as we discern the Radiant Forces with a new set of senses that I hope you will cultivate here.

There is more to time than what meets our senses.

There is more to our senses that can embrace time.

PART ONE

Soulful Preparations

Ode to Losing One's Self

Every story, if it is good, loses its author in it.

Nothing evolves without surrender.

At least the old self submits.

And that's when time really gets to work.

Events fly off the page.

Things happen.

Our feet get dirty and blistered crossing the
field.

We get wet wading across the river.

Some new strength stirs inside us.

The soul awakens.

~Joel B. Bennett (J.B.)

Imagine you are about to cross a wide and unknown field; one you have just come upon: the field of your happening life. Everything unfolds now in front of you as you take each step. This field of time is a health-producing gift, a helpful friend, and an intricate resource for living your life as fully as possible. To understand this gift, I ask you to consider that, at some level, this is not a book. Your life is not merely structured as in a book. You are crossing a field, then a river; you are lifted up, and other fields await.

You are endowed with a vital force that traverses this field of now. The contemplations that follow are designed to put you in touch with that vital force. In *QfP Book 1,* I described universal and cosmic forces that make the field come into being. You were not merely plopped down into this field of life. Instead, you emerged from it, are part of it, and embody those same forces that make up the field. Your essence knows the forces, the emerging field on your journey. Your soul works, plays, and awakens there.*

* This is the first of several dozen research notes that you will find referenced beginning on page 155. Other readers of this book suggested wanting these notes in the back of the book for easy reference but did not want to be interrupted by a citation note. From this point forward, I will not identify each research note, and you can certainly go to the Research Notes section anytime.

CHAPTER 1

Outside the Page

So much will bubble up between now and wherever it is that you are headed. The metaphor of your life as a book—words structured on a page, located in a chapter, situated within a section—is helpful. It is not ideal for the new approach to time developed here. A book is a conveyance, but it cannot carry you into the arms of destiny by itself. Reading and engaging the following activities will, I hope, help you fully befriend time and even make time your lover. And, the work happens *outside* the page. Therefore, let's call this an ongoing sharing, or offering, and not a book. Let me explain further.

The act of reading itself—as leisure, diversion, exploration—is its own time: a retreat, a time away from time, and possibly into the outskirts of that field. Reading for leisure, education, and self-help allows us to escape from the day, even for just a moment. "Life is a journey" is the more commonly used metaphor than "Life is a book." The word *journey* evolves from the original French-English word for "day" (*jour*), the same root as the word *journal*. Whether book or journey, our life is made of days that follow in sequence.

However, your life also includes Soulful Capacities that live outside of time, off the page. As such, the notion of "book," with its order of chapters and pages, can wed us to a view of time as linear, proceeding in a line from sunrise to sunset, from past to future. To experience time in a new and immersive way, I invite you to adopt the attitude that this is an offer to experience life, not a book of knowledge.

Indeed, our mental well-being may depend on this attitude. The ability to appreciate and savor life *as it is happening* is challenged by the digital barrage of pictures and information on the internet, where hyperlinks send readers in and out of websites. For many, it is more common to use hypermedia than to sit with, and savor, a singular book. Browsing the internet, one can follow endless branches from text to video to game to live event, social media, chat room, or video call in a seemingly random walk. We clamor for media attention in a world dedicated to distracting us. So, we mistake the whirl of information for the more exciting blur of this happening life.

The Boatman and the Scholar

There is an old fable about a boatman and a scholar. One day, the scholar needs to carry all of his books across the river. He starts to gossip with the simple boatman as they make their way across, asking how much the boatman has knowledge of astronomy and history and other fields of knowledge. The ordinary ferryman replies that his life requires no such knowledge; his routines are simple. The scholar starts to deride the boatman for all that he is missing out on, insinuating that the boatman's life is truly useless. Shortly after, the skies darken with thunder and lightning, and a severe thunderstorm rocks the boat. Just as the boat is about to capsize, the boatman asks the scholar if he knows how to swim. The scholar's face freezes with agony and fear, and the boatman innocently asks, "How useful are your books now?"

We might think that the main characters of this story are the boatman and the scholar. However, in this quest for presence, the river and the weather, the emerging elements of life, take center stage. To me, the story conveys the need to keep perspective. We have to be careful in criticizing those who lack what we hold as valuable. In another version of the story, the boatman may leave his ferried routine and venture out to the sea. In that circumstance, the scholar's knowledge of navigating the stars will keep the boatman from vanishing in uncharted waters. Both help the other appreciate and enrich their experience of life *as it unfolds*.

Your deeper, soulful self can resonate with and learn from many metaphors and stories. Hence, I use diverse methods to shake us loose from the illusion of time as just a tick-tocking, linear, relentlessness. In the coming pages, I offer a variety of modalities—poetry, research, questionnaires, stories, memoir, and writing exercises—through which to perceive time in a new way. I want you to be able to jump in and out, swim around, juke, jive, hover, take massive breaks, leave off, randomly walk, and pursue whatever style suits you. You are a scholar and a sailor and more.

Many come to this work seeking to tap into a sense and substance of presence within themselves. It is a quest for presence, for flow, and for meaning. Ironically, the quest typically begins in a protected and contained period (clock-time) that both helps and thwarts our ability to be present. This period—a segment of your life—often takes the form of a personal growth workshop, a retreat, a vision-seeking journey, a spiritual pilgrimage, a self-help book. All of these are sequenced frameworks. We can certainly learn *within* these times. But then, something happens.

What happens is LIFE. The move from naïve seeker to true initiate comes when the quest for presence becomes the immersion into whatever life throws at you, whether you're in a monastery or your car has broken down on the side of a highway in heavy traffic with no means of communication or thunder interrupts your voyage. Even the monk, with devotion to a pale routine, must deal with surprises, mishaps, and internal stirrings that become passions and then fires. This shift in attention—from *seeking* to *being*—can happen any time. Indeed, you are now (and now, and now) called to make the shift.

Time's Precious Tapestry

So, please accept this offer to shift and keep shifting your attention. See your life as a book, a journey, and more. Take the perspective of scholar, boatman, and others. Use any self-help or spiritual practice knowing that, on the one hand, your life will continue to happen after you practice and, on the other hand, the happening is itself the practice. Preciousness abides here, a time before and after the naïve seeker: a glimpse from innocence and death; the child who drinks the moment as life weaves about her; the revelations of the dying parent as everything weaves through and out of her.

"Time's Precious Tapestry" was the original title of this offering, the holy origin of both the quest and this happening life. When we stop long enough and look deep enough, we glimpse the shuttling threads of time's loom as it moves forward and back, up and down, and inside and out. We step off the mirage of the clock-time treadmill into an incredible web of life. And there we witness, either with awe or terror, just how brief our "time" seems.

Even clock-time, a purely human convenience, is part of this weave. Clocks seem necessary for this increasingly complex world. Paradoxically, society has grown increasingly complex *because* of clock-time or how business, economy, and technology manipulate it. We now have 24/7 workdays, the demise of Sunday or Sabbath respites, time pressures, time prisons, stress, burnout, exhaustion, sleeplessness, and addiction to everything and anything as a way to deal with the pressure.

The time we need to recover is not clock-time but rather the time of our own presence, our life now, and of the wonderful cosmos we are ever woven into. Join with me and lose yourself to find your soul. Get dirty crossing the field. Get wet crossing the river.

REFLECTION

Every talent, strength, or competency that leads to human achievement is fed by a deeper, soulful capacity for life itself. I once attended a spiritual retreat where I spent weeks in silence, only visiting with the meditation teacher once a week; and this was only for a brief visit to discuss the meditation practice. Meditating for up to fifteen hours a day, I lived an arid, monastic life. My experience of emotions, mental states, and consciousness itself grew very stark and very deep. I had to surrender to each moment. When the only thing that matters is paying attention with your heart, the world becomes utterly raw and terribly beautiful. Consciousness itself becomes precious.

The week approached for my return to the world. In that transition week, I could not meditate. Literally. Every time I sat down to quiet my mind I would start crying. Deep, gut-wrenching sobs would tear through my body, so much that I would tremble for minutes at a time. No words attached to this experience. All I knew was that the universe and my soul were going through some sort of temporary breakup. I could not return to the world, where an uncertain career, relationship difficulties, and my frail ego awaited me. I believed I lacked the skill or capacity to reestablish anything normal—that is, anything similar to the way "I" was before the retreat.

My experience of return was many years ago. Since then, in my struggle to "find myself in the world," I have studied many different aspects of human achievement. This includes studies of skills, aptitudes, strengths, and talents. The world is filled with wonderful guides. I have even written about them in two books I coauthored: *Heart-Centered Leadership* and *Your Best Self at Work*. We certainly benefit from guideposts and examples of other human beings who show us how to succeed in the time of our lives with its many challenges and opportunities.

But I have learned that the capacity for making it in life is quite different from the capacity for deeply experiencing, embracing, and appreciating our brief time here. In the vastness of time in the vastness of this universe, the human mind is less than a speck. Yet with Soulful Capacity, time itself becomes pliable and expandable. In those moments of deep sobbing—when my mind was empty except for a love of the cosmos and my soul's bond with it—I glimpsed a deeper well from which I could drink. All other human capacities come from the place of Capacity itself. A vast world swims within the speck that lies beyond our imagination. It informs everything we can ever hope to accomplish while we dwell here.

CHAPTER 2

Consciousness and the Soul

Ode to Soulful Capacities

There are no skills you have to learn.
Life will just bring them out of you.

You need wait for them no longer.
They have been incubating the whole time.

There is nothing new here for you.
Your soul knows all of this already.

So … why not just stop?
Let this wizard of a universe enchant you.

~J.B.

What do we mean by *soul* and related terms like *essence, spirit,* and *innermost being*? This chapter seeks to provide a definition that does not rely on a belief in the afterlife, reincarnation, angels, or the paranormal. You need not see yourself as religious or spiritual to make use of the concept of soul. All you need to believe is that you harbor a set of capacities, temporal competencies that you can become conscious of and that can be honed to uncover all life has to offer. If you have difficulty with the phrase "soulful capacity," then substitute the phrase "temporal competency" throughout this book. Before introducing these Soulful Capacities, this chapter begins to define what we mean by the terms "soul" and "consciousness."

One purpose of QfP is to help you find ways to become more empowered around a *deeper sense of time* than the one provided by culture, clock-time, and the 24/7 pace of life. Two fundamental ideas will help: the inevitable changes brought on by life itself and the ongoing interplay between our awareness and the universe.

First, we cannot escape the dance of life. Every moment, our body and our mind go through an array of changes such that each moment is special. This specialness is seen most clearly in small children. Every day, something fresh appears in their development: the ability to point, to use words, to name, to read, to solve problems, and so on. These changes continue on through and past adolescence into old age and until the moment of death. These later changes seem slower than those in childhood, so they are more difficult to discern. We change as we learn how to relate to others, how to love, how to master complex tasks, how to enjoy life, navigate old age, and approach death.

Second, these changes are a result of a deep and ongoing interplay between us—our brain, or mind/body system—and the rest of the universe. Recent developments in science suggest that our experience of the world around us is a projection of our consciousness. Simultaneously, our consciousness is a reflection of the world around us. The two cannot be separated. We inform the world, and the world informs us. The world unfolds as we experience it. Likewise, our actions shape how the world unfolds.

A central question of philosophy is "What is *it* that experiences this dance and unfolding?" *What* experiences both the mind (thoughts, emotions, colors) and the body (sensations, smells, tastes)? What makes us conscious? There are two key ideas involved here—consciousness and the soul. It is beyond the scope of this book to even summarize the vast and rich array of writings about soul and consciousness, writings that date back to the "beginning of history" in cultural, spiritual, and religious texts.

Our main purpose here is to understand these terms enough so we can enhance our approach to time as a health-giving resource. Some claim that, depending on our level of consciousness, clock-time can be either a prison for, a toy or playmate of, a brief diversion from, or an incidental distraction of the soul. We only need to find a livelihood and routine where we stay attracted to the quest, find ways of centering, and use clock-time as a resource rather than a preoccupation, slave-driver, or unhealthy distraction. Others claim that consciousness and the soul exist for the precise purpose of transcending time in all its forms—clock-time, seasons, etc.—altogether.

Consciousness

Consciousness is more than being aware and awake. We can be conscious even during sleep and, as discovered in research on *near-death experiences* (NDEs), even when the human brain is technically dead. Consciousness is a *superordinate concept*, or large cluster of concepts, that is notoriously difficult to define. A recent scientific review of twenty-nine theories of consciousness shows that most definitions of consciousness contain four components: experience, information, processes, and (mental) state. In your quest for presence, your focus is on the intimate and dancing relationship between these components.

The whole of consciousness is more than the sum of its component parts. I do not propose a final definition of consciousness. However, here is a working definition based on the scientific review mentioned above and recent thinking in the philosophy of the mind and *neurotheology* (or *spiritual neuroscience*):

Consciousness is both the wholeness of experience we feel and the dynamic or changing function of experience that emerges from and depends on information, processes, and mental states.

I use the word *processes* to refer to a series of actions or steps and so do not take place in an instant but unfold over time. The processes include:

1. feeling,

2. awareness,

3. some ability to control attention,

4. reference to space (objects and forms) and time (continuity and change), and

5. the interaction between a living being and information that resides in space and time; or, information that emerges as a function of the interaction.

Obviously, information and consciousness are intertwined. You would not have information without *attention* to the information. Also, it is through information that we attend. Consciousness informs, and information signals consciousness exists.

While consciousness is about experience, it is not, as the philosopher Sebastjan Vörös explains,

> *Something relegated to the "inside" of a human being that just represents the independent "outside" world. Instead, consciousness emerges in a dynamic interplay between the brain, body, and the world. A living being, in constituting itself as a living being, enacts its own world; that is, its own field of significance and meaning, and it is against the background of this circular (two-way) interaction that consciousness emerges.* (Vörös, 2014).

Consciousness—also called sentience—requires a living being. Yet, many who have NDEs claim that their consciousness exists apart from their body. These NDEs include out-of-body experiences, pleasant feelings, and visions including a tunnel, a light, deceased relatives, or a life review. Scientists argue that NDEs may be completely understood in terms of brain neurophysiology.

Dr. Pim van Lommel has argued that there is no study confirming that consciousness is solely a function of the brain. Dr. van Lommel, among others, has studied many individuals who had an NDE during a transient loss of all functions of the cortex and the brainstem. In nearly every case, individuals' lives are permanently changed. Their memory of the NDE was "more real" than other recalled experiences: clearer, more intense, and more contextual in terms of remembering location and arrangement of people.

Soul

By almost every definition, the soul is a beautiful thing. There is an abundance of beautiful and complex images of the soul from ancient civilizations. For example, in ancient Indian texts, there is truly one soul; each human being has that soul within them. Ancient Greek writers placed the soul in the heart. Egyptian beliefs saw the soul as having many parts, including the heart and intellect, and physical, spiritual, and other aspects.

An Atheist's View

The more I have understood about how the universe works, the more that awe has come, and the more joy. Rather than going, "Oh, that's all just *clockwork*. The sun is there and we go around it every year. And all that stuff." No, I think, "That is Amazing!" It is extraordinary how that has *happened*." (emphases added)

~*ROBERT LLEWELLYN, writer, TV presenter, speaker, actor (Red Dwarf), electric vehicle evangelist.*

Pre-Hispanic Mayans viewed the soul and name as the same and held that individuals had many souls. One translation of *soul* in Mayan hieroglyphics is "white-flower-thing." Below I describe Western and more modern definitions of soul. By way of contrast, here is an edited description from an ancient Hindu text, The Maha Narayana Upanishad (verse XIII-9-11).

Inside the center of the heart,
There is an ever-shining fire,
Which is spread in all directions,
And that fire which burns stable,

Sees everywhere,
Never gets old…

Like the dazzling sparkle of lightning,
From within a black dark cloud,
Like the sprout of a red paddy,
Slender and golden,
And as tiny as an atom
That flame continues burning.

(Combined translations from Swami Vimalananda and P. R. Ramachander)

Modern scientific studies, like those of NDEs, are complex and controversial, and yet they also offer a functional definition of soul. You may consider yourself religious or spiritual, or you may be an atheist. You may believe only in hard science and observable data. Yet even atheists have feelings of awe and transcendence (see quote by Robert Llewellyn). You may be more open-minded and believe in the unobservable realities described by quantum physics and holographic views of the universe. Research shows that most people believe in a soul—an innermost aspect of one's being that differs from opinions, ideas, attitudes, ego, and personality, something that transcends a current self or personality. For many, this aspect of the soul also transcends time; it existed before we were born and will continue after we die.

In the study of Western philosophy, many definitions of the soul are derived from Aristotle. In essence, Aristotle defines the soul as *what exists within a living thing that is responsible for and animates the activities of that living thing.* More recently, writers explain the soul or essence in diverse ways. Here is a sample of definitions. I also recommend the work of Gary Zukav and Thomas Moore (see Research Notes).

✦ *A. H. Almaas.* A. H. Almaas defines "essence" as our true self, fully present to experience, in contact with reality, confident, and having a timeless sense of being complete and whole, lacking nothing.

Almaas contrasts this true self from the false self of ego, which gets attached to or fixates on certain beliefs and views out of a sense of lack or incompleteness.

+ *Ken Wilber.* The philosopher Ken Wilber explains that the soul exists at different levels of consciousness or has different layers. We should be careful about defining the soul because our definition may be based on only one level. Wilber assumes that within each person is the capacity to experience transpersonal consciousness, that is, the expansion of our mind beyond human consciousness. It is within these outer limits that the soul exists, and it changes and develops as it traverses the various levels of consciousness. For example, we move from seeing ourselves only as a separate and singular being to seeing ourselves through the eyes of collective humanity. We can move from identifying only with our personal beliefs and dramas to seeing ourselves as having a sense of unity with all humanity. The soul is not a static entity. It metamorphizes and emerges as our consciousness changes. Wilber states, "At the bottom of your soul is the soul of humanity itself, but a divine, transcendent soul, leading from bondage to liberation, from enchantment to awakening, from time to eternity, from death to immortality" (Wilber, 1979, p.124).

+ *Abraham Maslow.* Abraham Maslow distinguished self-transcendence (the ability to move beyond one's own limited viewpoint to embrace selfless and universal aspects of being; see chapter 9) from self-actualization (coming into a full and deep sense of self). Scientists have studied self-transcendence and have developed several short questionnaires. For example, consider the self-transcendence subscale of the "Temperament and Character Inventory (TCI)," developed by Dr. C. Robert Cloninger. Along with similar measures, the TCI contains survey statements that describe decreased self-salience and increased feelings of connectedness. Sample items include "My individual life is a part of a greater whole" and "The events in my life unfold according to a divine or greater plan."

A modern definition views the soul as a neuronal-synaptic signature of information that integrates brain and body through a complex electrochemical flow of neurotransmitters. This neural signature, unique for each of us, manifests in daily experiences of insight, spirituality, or epiphanies. As the universe is itself made of information, our soul continues on as part of the warp and weave of information throughout the cosmos. We can touch into this more often than we might otherwise think.

This quick review reveals that most definitions of soul, essence, or self-transcendence involve a sense of and drive toward wholeness and timelessness—that is, a sense that one's entire being exists outside of the timeframe of one's life. At a basic level, many human beings can discern an inner self that is truer, more enduring, and more connected to others and the universe than what exists through the lens of their individual self or personality.

A Definition of the Soul (Rather than Defining the Soul)

Awareness of the soul requires consciousness of something that lives *outside* of space and time, is often ineffable or beyond language, is immaterial, and is connected to or part of the universe. Given the diverse definitions above and the sense that the soul's experience transcends language, I believe we can offer a definition of the soul rather than define, that is, limit, the soul. Accordingly, I offer this definition:

> *The soul is that inherent, unified, and whole aspect of a living being that contains or enfolds information from the entire universe.*
>
> *The soul exists outside time and also (a) connects the past to the future, (b) connects the current embodiment of the living being to all past and future representations or incarnations of that being, (c) is accessible through and animates consciousness, and (d) evolves and unfolds through the experience of the inherent, unified, and whole connection provided by (a), (b), and (c).*

Distinctions follow from the above definitions of consciousness and the soul. Consciousness is the *actual* manifestation or use of attention and awareness, whereas the soul is always an entity with *potential.* The soul is capacious: It has enormous space or room within which consciousness can roam. Consciousness refers to awareness of objects and forms that both abide and change in time, whereas soul can transcend space and time. Consciousness, because it involves attention, is something we can sometimes focus or control, whereas the soul underlies and animates consciousness. That is, the soul provides the energy and *ability* for consciousness to arise and to be focused or controlled. Presence is the coming together of consciousness and the soul.

> *Presence is the coming together of consciousness and the soul.*

We can become conscious of the soul through self-transcendence. When alert and fully interacting with space and time, we can access information we were not previously aware of. That is, features of the universe emerge as we interact with it. One of those features is the current embodiment of our being that enfolds information from the entire universe. The soul does not only reside within us. We can experience it through the world and environment around us.

This last claim is supported by numerous studies on the varieties of religious, transcendent, conversion, and/or peak experiences. These are studies and reviews, beyond those of NDEs, that include more mundane revelations that can occur to individuals regardless of their religious orientation and whether or not they maintain a spiritual or meditative practice. Hence, it is possible to experience soul at any time in the world around us or, more clearly, in the ways we perceive and interact with the world.

On Gratitude

For many people, the experience and feeling of gratitude touches or awakens the soul. Of all the soulful experiences we can have, gratitude is perhaps the one we most discuss in common or daily social life. Gratitude often points to being thankful *for something* that has happened in the past; a gift, receiving service, or support from others. We can experience appreciation or thankfulness for a kind gesture, a teacher, or the generosity of others. We can also feel a deep sense of gratitude for having escaped a challenge, adversity, or trauma—and even for having endured each of these. Finally, at some point, we may experience an all-encompassing gratitude for being born as a human being. Most spiritual teachings call us into this deep appreciation. Gratitude can range across the moment, for an occasion, from a trial, or for our entire existence.

It is this last experience—having a deep abiding value and treasuring for just being alive—that we highlight here. My experience of time is transformed in the moment of such gratitude, and the quest for presence becomes essential. I move beyond acceptance and into being present *with something outside myself,* something that lasts longer than my own thoughts about myself. I pause to receive. In receiving, I glimpse that I am part of a wider fabric of selfless exchange.

Research on the measurement of gratitude and appreciation suggests that they both have an intrinsic relationship with time. Measures include items like these:

✦ I stop and enjoy my life as it is.

✦ I think it's really important to "stop and smell the roses."

✦ Thinking about dying reminds me to live every day to the fullest.

Practicing gratitude on a daily basis supports our quest. As you self-assess your Soulful Capacities in the next sections, notice how gratitude plays a role in each of them. For example, can there be gratitude without Acceptance? Gratitude either awakens our Presence to the other from whom the gift comes, or it calls us to presence with them. For example, I am deeply and *forever* grateful for teachers, helpers, and therapists I have had in my life. Recalling what they did for me, I often feel that I was not as present as I could have been. Gratitude for others makes me want to be more present to them.

The more I appreciate what I have been given, especially in the daily tasks of life, the more likely I am to Flow with them and have even more spontaneous gratitude. Flow, harmony, and cooperation are more likely in Gratitude—alone and together with others—than when we begrudge or resist our responsibilities. Finally, Synchronicity and appreciation go hand in hand. Synchronicity may be the highest form of gratitude. The more we practice gratitude for everything that happens, the more likely everything that happens holds a purpose, meaning, and fulfillment that we may not see until the serendipitous moment in which it happens.

The Soulful Capacities

We can now turn to those aforementioned temporal competencies, or capacities innate within the soul, that give us the ability to experience the Treasures of this happening life. That is, the Soulful Capacities help us to become *conscious*, to *connect*, to *evolve*, and to *unfold*. They allow us to *capture and process information enfolded within the precious weave of time*.

QfP Book 5: The Treasures goes into detail on these different types of experiences, organizing them to help you better recognize when they occur. These experiences are more likely to occur, or we are more likely to access them, when we develop or cultivate our Soulful Capacities. That is what the Soulful Capacities are, in part, designed to do.

Special Temporal Nature of Soulful Capacities

There are many Soulful Capacities. In the back of this book, you will find a list of more of them, along with helpful synonyms for those that are not already described here. The four I delve into—Acceptance, Presence, Flow, and Synchronicity—are unique states in which the mind touches the soul, where we live more deeply in the moment-to-moment unfolding of life. As the journey of the soul is itself beyond time, the capacities give the mind access to eternal processes and then frame them within clock-time in ways that can be appreciated through the awakening of the soul. The capacities are like windows into the soul.

They also support us from moment to moment. Through them, we enhance our orientation to time in ways that support our well-being. The quality of attentional effort or focus differs for each of them. How we bring our energy and effort to our perception of time helps shape our experience of these capacities. They are not just mental states. They come from a deeper place of wholeness and connection. They are of the soul.

With Acceptance, our attention becomes spacious, detached, and allowing. Time takes on the quality of spaciousness; our effort is relaxed and sustained. With Presence, our focus is more substantive, immediate, pointed, and discovering. Time broadens, heightens, and reveals. Our effort is more involved and somatic, connected to sensation and substance. With Flow, our attention itself proceeds into time, but then our sense of time subsides as we recruit our intentions and muscles to interact with the world and the task at hand. We intrinsically enjoy the effort for effort's sake. With Synchronicity, we are caught off guard, sidelined, resonating and reverberating. Times takes on the quality of something bigger than ourselves; the whole experience has nothing to do with our effort at all.

Using Research Notes with Soulful Capacity

Scientific research has explored each of the different Soulful Capacities, or aspects of them, to varying degrees. In the next chapters, I will mention or refer to this research for the purpose of supporting your quest. Please explore the Research Notes section for detailed references. When you do, attempt to bring the quality of that Soulful Capacity to the task of looking up the reference. Be curious as a function of self-acceptance. Maintain Presence as you follow one reference to another and possibly meander through the research literature. You might even enter a Flow state where time disappears as you discover some insight, make a poignant connection between ideas, or see the big picture. Or observe Synchronicity: you find the very thing you have been looking for just in that moment when you decide to follow the untraveled path.

Contemplation (QfP 2-1)*:
Consciousness and the Soul

Reflect upon the ideas in this chapter by first writing these words on a blank page:

> Gratitude, Soul, Soulful Capacity,
> Time Competency, Consciousness,
> Near-Death Experiences

Of all these, Gratitude may be the most familiar idea. Ask yourself:

✦ How often do I spontaneously experience Gratitude in my life? Am I grateful for just being alive?

✦ Do I practice Gratitude?

✦ How does Gratitude connect to, reflect, or help me understand the other ideas?

- Specifically, how does the experience of Gratitude involve or require my soul?

---

* Each contemplation in all of the books in the QfP collection is also found in the workbook companion. To help find these, we use the notation of QfP #-# to designate the Book and the Contemplation within the book. Hence, this first Contemplation QfP 2-1 is the first Contemplation in Book 2.

- How does the experience of Gratitude indicate some capacity within me to touch into or give expression to my soul or soulful nature? Or,

- Is soul even involved? Is gratitude more a competency toward time—my ability to return to living in the present moment?

✦ How is Gratitude a window into consciousness and the soul?

✦ What is my own experience with death, dying, or near-death?

Consider this key question for journaling:

What is my own capacity for experiencing the soul?

PART TWO

The Soulful Capacities

A Preview

Accepting the moment, we can become present
    to the occasion of our life;

Our Presence within this occasion allows us to
    Flow with whatever unfolds next;

We become fully alive in between these
    unfoldings and the unique way we enfold
    the Treasures of life within our personality,

The Whole-Time.

CHAPTER 3

Acceptance

Ode to Acceptance

All is mind. And after that, essence.
Abide in "this is that."
Abide in "thou art that."
With equanimity.
Allowing spaciousness,
You will arrive.

Then, let the ordinary
capture and release you.

Just as a flower
closes at dusk and
opens at dawn.

Tát Tvam Ási.
Jai Guru Deva.

~J.B.

Acceptance: the most fundamental competency on our path of time empowerment and likely of all enlightenment. This includes Acceptance of events around us, our status in life, our emotions, our mental and physical limitations, our thoughts, and especially our reactions and judgment of ourselves and others. An open-minded and curious quality of everything that is happening in the moment is the basis of mindfulness. We practice this attitude when sitting alone in meditation. And, it can be cultivated with a loving and caring family member, friend, life coach, or therapist.

Day-to-day hassles often challenge Acceptance, yet it is in these ordinary events where Acceptance shines. Acceptance calls us to live one day at a time, to let go, be patient, and witness how wonderful life is, just as it is—and to be fulfilled by it. The greatest calls to Acceptance come from having to face the sudden loss of a loved one, an unexpected failure, a debilitating disease, the loss of physical and mental function, and death. Grief and Acceptance work together in healing.

Acceptance also means self-acceptance. There has been quite a lot of research on self-acceptance. This includes work in counseling psychology in the 1940s, associated with the humanistic psychologist Carl Rogers and his notion of unconditional positive self-regard. This is an attitude of responding to oneself and others with Acceptance, empathy, and support, regardless of what is said or done. We see ourselves as a "work in progress," relaxing any perfectionism, promoting self-kindness as a value, and seeing ourselves from multiple perspectives.

Among the challenges to Acceptance are living in our head, holding on to resentments, clinging to our own made-up stories of what should happen (overcontrolling) or what could happen (anxiety), and having negative thoughts about ourselves or others. When we resist accepting, it is almost always because we get caught up in the unhelpful mental states described in *QfP Book 1*: worrying about the past, trying to overmanage the future, being anxious about the unpredictable, and ruminating or engaging in repeated and negative self-talk.

Let the words of my mouth and the meditation of my heart
be acceptable in your sight, O Lord.

~Psalm 19:14 (NKJV)

It is possible to cultivate Acceptance through the exercises provided below. However, if you have experienced significant trauma, abuse, or violence; have lived an unhealthy and overstressed lifestyle; or have thoughts of suicide, I encourage you to also reach out for help.

Before attempting the exercises below please review these two quotes from teachers whose careers have been dedicated to helping others develop consciousness of our essence. The first quote emphasizes the difference between how things are and how we want them to be and the quality of curiosity. Sincere curiosity is an aspect of consciousness that brings our soul into life. The second emphasizes the difference between the wakefulness of Acceptance and the sleep of giving up. I chose these two quotes because they succinctly convey the core features of Acceptance.

> *The practice of self-observation begins with a desire and resolution on your part: "I want to know what really is, regardless of how I prefer things to be ..." It is important that self-observation become associated with our essential curiosity and the inherent joy of that curiosity.*
>
> ~CHARLES T. TART, PhD (AMERICAN PSYCHOLOGIST KNOWN FOR HIS WRITING WITHIN THE STUDY OF CONSCIOUSNESS AND ALTERED STATES OF CONSCIOUSNESS, AND ONE OF THE FOUNDERS OF THE FIELD OF TRANSPERSONAL PSYCHOLOGY)

> *Acceptance isn't wimping out. Accepting the circumstances of your life is sometimes misunderstood as wimping out, knuckling under, or giving up—but, in fact, it's just the opposite ... if you face your situation squarely and get the help you need to heal your past, then the devil will do a disappearing act.*
>
> ~JOAN BORYSENKO, PhD (AMERICAN SCIENTIST, LICENSED PSYCHOLOGIST, SPIRITUAL DIRECTOR, AND PIONEER IN THE FIELD OF INTEGRATIVE MEDICINE)

Exercises

With each Soulful Capacity, or temporal competency, you will have at least two exercises that can be completed with journaling or with a group. These and other exercises offered here are best seen as starting places, designed to give you a direct experience of the capacity. They are not a substitute for ongoing, regular, and dedicated practice. For example, you can form a study group that makes a long-term commitment to work these exercises. You can use the accompanying workbook for the QfP and start a daily practice where you dedicate time every day or every weekend to do at least one exercise.

The first exercise asks you to reflect on quotations and answer some questions about them for yourself and, possibly, with others. The second exercise is a quick survey or self-assessment you can use to gauge the degree to which the capacity is accessible or alive in you right now. Your score on this and all other assessments is not a diagnosis or indication of whether you have the capacity (because you most certainly do). It is only a momentary reflection—based on your ratings—of how much you are in touch with that capacity.

In each of these exercises, the important thing to remember is the *process* of reflection rather than the outcome of sharing. We are all on this journey, both alone and together. By allowing a safe space—giving yourself time for reflection—there is a very good chance that you will get in touch with your own inner wisdom. Allow your thoughts and feelings to wander a little. It is very important that you create an environment of Acceptance for anything that surfaces. In fact, we access all of the Soulful Capacities *through the process of Contemplation.*

Guidelines for All Soulful Capacity Exercises

1. Before doing an exercise, please take one minute to sit quietly and allow your breathing to become steady and relaxed. You can close your eyes.

2. After one minute, repeat in a calm and compassionate voice: "I love and accept myself just as I am. I love and accept myself with all my faults and shortcomings."

3. Make sure the pace is steady and not rushed. For example, for the quotation exercise, open your eyes to read or (if in a group) hear someone read. Keep the pace of reading steady and not rushed, and include a pause between each statement.

4. Allow the practice to wash over you. Allow the words to connect with an innermost part of you—a quality memory, a cherished value, a deeply held aspiration, or a spiritual longing.

5. Stay still and notice what happens with your feelings and in your body before trying to make sense of it, write something down, or share your ideas.

Contemplation (QfP 2-2): Acceptance

Acceptance Exercise 1: Quotation Reflection

After taking a few minutes to get quiet, centered, and in a contemplative mood, please reflect on each of these quotations one at a time.

*The moment you accept what troubles
you have been given, a door opens.*

~MAWLANA JALALUDDIN MUHAMMAD RUMI
(SUFI POET, MYSTIC)

*Whether it is the best of times or the worst
of times, it is the only time we have.*

~ART BUCHWALD (AMERICAN HUMORIST)

*Life is a series of natural and spontaneous changes. Don't
resist them; that only creates sorrow. Let reality be reality.*

~LAO TZU (TAOIST SAGE)

*The ache for home lives in all of us. The safe place
where we can go as we are and not be questioned.*

~MAYA ANGELOU (AMERICAN POET)

God grant me the serenity to accept
the things I cannot change ...

~THE SERENITY PRAYER (REINHOLD NIEBUHR,
AMERICAN THEOLOGIAN)

So much of our anguish is created when we are in resistance.
So much relief, release, and change are possible when
we accept, simply accept ... Acceptance turns us into the
person we are and want to be. Acceptance empowers the
events and circumstances to turn around for the better.

~MELODY BEATTIE (AMERICAN AUTHOR OF SELF-HELP BOOKS)

Accept that some days you're the pigeon,
and some days you're the statue.

~ROGER C. ANDERSON (COLLEGE PRESIDENT, AUTHOR)

Acceptance Exercise 2:
Questions for Journaling or Discussion

1. Which of the above quotations spoke to you the most?

2. Which one reminded you of any current challenge you have with taking things in stride or letting go, being patient, or relaxing amid any urgency you have?

3. Reflecting on your answers, what do you notice about your internal chatter, your own story, or your need to have things be a certain way?

4. What other quotations, stories, or examples from your own life teach you to be more accepting?

5. What are the gifts of Acceptance?

6. What, if any, steps do you want to take to remind yourself about Acceptance?

Acceptance Exercise 3: Self-Assessment

There are two sections to this assessment. For both sections, you will rate each statement on a five-point scale from "Rarely true about me" to "Often true about me." The first section lists statements that are worded in a positive direction and indicate more capacity for Acceptance. The second lists statements worded in a less positive direction. Both sections are important. As you make your selections, make sure you note the rating value (1 to 5 or 5 to 1) and that the values are different for each section.

This self-assessment—and the others that follow for Flow, Presence, and Synchronicity—make up one part of the *Quest for Presence Inventory*™, with the other segment contained in *QfP Book 3*. After you complete all four of the Soulful Capacity self-assessments, you will have an opportunity to summarize your scores and contemplate them as a whole in chapter 12.

This statement is true ...	Rarely	Some-times	In Between	Usually	Often
1. I accept and approve of myself just as I am.	1	2	3	4	5
2. I can forgive myself for things I have done.	1	2	3	4	5
3. When I have distressing thoughts or images, I am able to just notice them without reacting.	1	2	3	4	5
4. I perceive my emotions without having to react to them.	1	2	3	4	5
5. I am patient with myself when I encounter challenging tasks.	1	2	3	4	5
6. I am able to be patient with others I dislike or who bother me.	1	2	3	4	5
7. I tolerate aspects of my personality I may not always like.	1	2	3	4	5
8. It is better to let things go than to try and pick my battles.	1	2	3	4	5
9. I am able to just enjoy the simple and ordinary things in life.	1	2	3	4	5
10. I feel a sense of fulfillment from just allowing life to happen.	1	2	3	4	5
11. I get down on myself or my past more often than I want to.	5	4	3	2	1
12. I obsess about upcoming situations or projects.	5	4	3	2	1
13. I am bothered by anxiety.	5	4	3	2	1
14. I am a perfectionist.	5	4	3	2	1

This statement is true …	Rarely	Some-times	In Between	Usually	Often
15. I blow things out of proportion.	5	4	3	2	1
16. It is difficult for me to just sit quietly with the passing day.	5	4	3	2	1
17. I am easily irritated by some people.	5	4	3	2	1
18. In my close relationships, I more likely argue or react than let the other person have their say.	5	4	3	2	1
19. Once I get angry, it is hard for me to calm down.	5	4	3	2	1
20. I often strive to get what I want rather than learn to take the good with the bad in life.	5	4	3	2	1

After you have completed rating all twenty items, please total your scores. The total score you could receive ranges from 20 to 100. The score you receive can change from time to time, so please check back and rate yourself on these items as often as you would like. This is not a test designed to pigeonhole you in a particular personality "type" or to help you diagnose any problem you might have. Instead, treat it as an opportunity to reflect on how much, right now in this moment, you have access to this attitude of Acceptance. For this reason, I suggest you refrain from comparing your score with others or judging yourself in any way. That would defeat the purpose of the exercise. Just notice what score you have today. Be with that. Accept that.

Self-Assessment Questions for Journaling or Discussion

1. What are your internal and emotional reactions to the score you received?

2. Do you notice more of a tendency to quickly react to the score or more of a tendency to just sit with and process the meaning of the score?

3. Which of the twenty statements caused you most to think, "This is me," or really captured your current level of Acceptance? Explain why.

4. Which one reminded you of any current challenge you have with taking things in stride or letting go, being patient, or relaxing amid any urgency you have?

5. Reflecting on your answers, what do you notice about your internal chatter, your own story, or your need to have things be a certain way?

6. What are your core strengths of Acceptance?

7. What appears to be getting in the way of Acceptance?

8. What, if any, steps do you want to take to remind yourself about Acceptance?

REFLECTION

My Acceptance came from my love to swim. I loved it so much that when I toured through Europe, I would take time in each location—Amsterdam, Copenhagen, Stockholm, Munich, Ventimiglia, Venice—for a half-mile or mile of lap swimming for daily exercise. Around the time of this trip, I started feeling tired a lot and had symptoms that the doctor thought reflected Lyme disease. Despite testing, there was no definitive diagnosis. A few years later, I got really sick and lay in bed for a week with a fever. My symptoms included paralysis in my shoulders and upper arms. I could not move my arms away from my torso in any direction, and I could barely bend my elbows. The doctor could find no explanation for my symptoms. I was, at the time, living in Winona, Minnesota, near Rochester, the home of the Mayo Clinic. The team of neurologists put me through an intensive battery of tests, including electromyography, spinal tap, and other exams. In the end, they could not diagnose my condition, labeling it "idiopathic brachial plexopathy." This essentially means that the nerves that serve my upper-arm muscles were not working for a reason of unknown origin.

It took almost two years to regain the use of these muscles. I could swim but not without fatiguing quickly. Many gifts stem from this experience. A lack of diagnosis deepened my sense of mystery: not everything needs explanation. While I could not use my arms, I still could use my hands and fingers. And since my plexopathy, I have written many articles and books. Most of all, the upper arms have symbolized spiritual wings for me. Instead of focusing on their external use, my time in recovery led me to meditate on the inner meaning of my soul as it learned to "swim" through this and other challenges with acceptance. Indeed, when I get in touch with my "spiritual wings," it is easier for me to accept challenges and sweat less the small stuff.

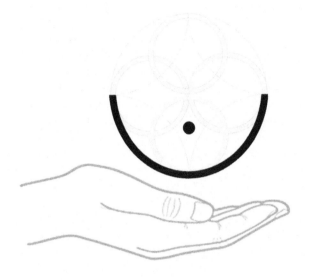

All is Acceptance

CHAPTER 4

Presence

Ode to Presence

All is secure. And after that, void.
Abide in that awe.
Abide in "I am that I am" [יְהֶוֶה]

With harmony, wonder, and affection.
Show up.
Fully.
Omnipresent.

Then, be with
the coherence of it all.

Just as the earth's axis
watches the seasons,
the starry swirls,
the darkness filling up.

~J.B.

Presence is a relaxed but also energized ability to be fully attentive to your whole self and your surroundings. It includes the sense of inner warmth, glow, or strength. In presence, you know that your core being is whole and vibrant. Presence is often fueled by having a sense of purpose and meaning in one's life, a desire to be authentic and honest, and the motivation to live life in accordance with deeply held values. It requires intention and an agile ability to willfully direct your awareness into the heart of the moment. It requires a willingness to be completely truthful about yourself. Your presence can change an ordinary, unnoticed moment into a moment of beauty that can feed the soul.

Life energy imbues Presence with many rich qualities. Mentally, you fully engage with your own thoughts and feelings, and physically, your whole body can be present or fully immersed in the world. Presence can also be spiritual: You sense a connection, resonance, or coherence to your world; a deep connection to nature; in your relationships with others; and even to the universe. This is felt as awe, wonder, and humility.

Present awareness can move between a highly focused attention to details (for example, colors, musical notes, textures, aroma) to a wide lens, an almost 360-degree view of the environment (such as hiking a mountain trail, performing in a sport). Further, Presence involves fully feeling one's emotions. We have a spacious ability to be with the complete range and duration of feelings: joy, sadness, anger, fear, longing, affection. One can even be fully aware of one's own tiredness or fatigue.

Research on Presence includes four different areas. This includes the Presence of caregivers or doctors during the provider-client interaction and the importance and ethical obligation of being present as a practice. In the field of virtual reality and simulations, scientists study how much the user feels actual Presence within the simulation. Studies in spirituality and in bereavement talk about a sense of spiritual Presence and a sense of one's departed loved one being present. Finally, a self-assessment measure of *psychological absorption* is used in research in consciousness and hypnosis. Individuals who score high on this measure show a quality of deep involvement with the objects of consciousness, the abilities to get deeply immersed in an activity, and surrender or become totally absorbed in what is happening.

Many self-guided practices help to cultivate Presence, including meditation, mantra, prayer, yoga, pottery, contemplative dance, Tai

Chi, and Qigong. These and other more action-oriented practices can require us to perform with a heightened sense of awareness. This includes martial arts, archery, surfing, musicianship, and all competitive sports and the performing arts. These practices may or may not require any tool, instrument, or equipment. If they do, the tool requires handling and manipulating in ways that involves dexterity and often full use of our torso and limbs.

We also can practice Presence through close work with others, as mentioned above, through coaching, counseling, nursing, and psychotherapy. And Presence is activated through hobbies like crafting, painting, mandala art, calligraphy, gardening, knitting, landscaping, and woodworking. To a certain extent, artful conversation, public speaking, and competitive debate requires Presence in the form of skillful vigilance in speech, sentence structure, and word usage.

With these practices, one starts with the mechanics of routine (learning the moves, memorizing, rote repetition). Later, one develops mastery, artistry, or expertise. The shift from routine to mastery is core to understanding Presence. We are present when we fully connect to what we are doing. We entrain *with*, are in sync *with*, or couple our awareness *with* the practice. For example, in Zen archery, the archer, the bow, the arrow, and the target all become one in that precise moment the arrow is released. The following two quotations convey two additional aspects of Presence that are important to highlight. The first reminds us that just by letting go of thinking and the complications of life, we naturally rest in Presence. The second reminds us that we need not do anything to experience Presence, and Presence may actually arise through nonaction.

> *Resting in simple presence is so foreign to a*
> *lifelong habit of mental complication ... we may*
> *be overwhelmed by how vast and free life suddenly*
> *feels when our minds are not on the hunt.*

~CATHERINE INGRAM (FROM *PASSIONATE PRESENCE:*
EXPERIENCING THE SEVEN QUALITIES OF AWAKENED AWARENESS)

*Without doing anything, things can sometimes go
more smoothly just because of our peaceful presence.
In a small boat when a storm comes, if one person
remains solid and calm, others will not panic,
and the boat is more likely to stay afloat.*

~MACRINA WIEDERKEHR (FROM *A TREE FULL OF ANGELS:
SEEING THE HOLY IN THE ORDINARY*)

Challenges to Presence

The most basic challenges to Presence are distraction, distractibility,
or getting lost in the distraction; overthinking; and busyness. We fall
off the path. This is in contrast to Acceptance, where the challenge
is resistance and getting caught up in worry and rumination. We
can notice these states. It is the continual return—notice and come
back—that is the heart of Presence. We also set up healthy boundaries, becoming vigilant. We do not allow ourselves to get drawn into
the distraction. When we do, we simply notice what is happening and
return to the present.

Beyond the challenge of distraction, four types of obstacles lie
on the path of Presence: the unhelpful mental states themselves; the
trappings of culture, media, and technology; doubt or low levels of
confidence; and addiction. To deal with each of these, the first step is
to go back to Acceptance, acknowledge they are problems, and do so
without judgment. Tell yourself, "Yes, of course, these are distractions.
There is nothing wrong with me because I get distracted. It makes
sense." The second step is self-compassion. Tell yourself, "I care about
myself and my ability to be present in my life. I can be patient and
loving as I redirect my awareness."

We have discussed the unhelpful mental states in the section
above on Acceptance. Please refer back to that section for practices
that may be helpful. In addition, a distinct practice of Presence can
give you the physical energy, endurance, and stamina you need to stay

focused when negative thoughts arise. Here is a brief review of the other challenges to Presence.

External Trappings of Culture, Media, and Technology: Throughout history, teachers of presence have always warned about the distractions of the marketplace and their appeal to base instincts of desire, lust, and attachment to impermanent, superficial, and material fascinations. In today's commercial world, these distractions have grown in quantity and sophistication. The comedian George Carlin had a great routine where he calls this "stuff" (Cohan, 2008).

> *That's all your house is, it's a place to keep your*
> *stuff while you go out and get more stuff.*
> ~GEORGE CARLIN (AMERICAN COMEDIAN)

Social media, electronic mail, the use of smartphones, gaming, and continuous advertisements are all a function of a sped-up, 24/7, time-imprisoned matrix that we allow ourselves to get caught in and identified with. In fact, the word *media* itself indicates that there is something in between us—a medium—that does not allow us to be fully present to each other. Whenever we get drawn into electronic applications, our Presence diminishes and even can vanish.

Most important, consider how we are reduced to using only our fingertips on glass screens to interact with the mobile and computer technology through push-button apps, while in the Presence practices named above, we must engage the full body. Tell yourself, "I am present first and foremost to my own life, my precious time, and those I love. I am not my identity on social media. I let go of any unhelpful need to have electronics. I let go of all distractions that do not serve me."

In Presence practices, we engage
the full body.

Doubt or Low Self-Confidence: Doubt is bound to creep up on anyone who struggles with Presence. Just reflect on both the internal and external distractions we just reviewed. There are incessant distractions. The key is to see each distraction as an opportunity rather than as an obstacle. Indeed, every time you notice a distraction and see it for what it is, you already have begun to win the war for Presence. Taking the attitude of "The obstacle is the way" is not only the basis of Presence but also resilience. Your attention is made stronger each time you face the demon of doubt. Tell yourself, "I am capable of anything I set my mind to. I am powerful in my attentiveness. I now move forward and embrace the present moment."

Addiction: The science of recovery from addiction has grown significantly in recent years. We now have greater understanding of the brain mechanisms that underlie addiction. Often, the first step for someone suffering from a compulsion or dependency is to recognize that they are a human being with an addiction rather than an addiction that has seized a human being. In other words, recovery from addiction requires practicing self-acceptance and being present to negative self-talk sequences involving shame, guilt, doubt, and other self-judgments. There are many affirmations that help with addiction. The 12-step programs have dozens of slogans that are used in meetings and sponsors; some examples: *This too shall pass, One day at a time, How important is it, Keep it simple,* and *Progress, not perfection.*

It is difficult to resolve an addiction on one's own without three key resources: (1) the help of a supportive community, support group, or therapist; (2) the ability to persevere and stick to it over a period of several months; and (3) some set of values or principles that place importance on health, service, community, and the recovery process itself. These resources are, in fact, core to any work on Presence.

Contemplation (QfP 2-3): Presence

As above with the Acceptance exercises, there is both a set of quotations to reflect upon and a self-assessment. But first, I recommend to do two physical or somatic awareness exercises. The first exercise asks you to get in touch with the Presence of your heart and heartbeat. The second asks you to be mindful of your body as you move. Be sure to refer to the "Guidelines for All Soulful Capacity Exercises" described in chapter 3.

Presence Exercise 1: Heart Awareness

Sit on a chair or comfortably on a couch or cushion so your back is straight but also relaxed. Take a few minutes to get quiet. Follow these steps in a paced way.

1. Place your right hand over your heart, adjusting its position until you sense your heartbeat. Leave your hand there for a minute. Allow thoughts or body sensations to come and go, each time returning your attention to the heartbeat.

2. As you relax, allow the palm of your hand to feel warm, supple, and deeply relaxed. It is almost as though it melts into or merges with your chest. Let a minute pass as you experience this.

3. Take your other hand and cup it over your right hand. Let it rest lightly over the right hand. Note the sensation that you are gently

holding or hugging yourself with a sense of care. Allow any feelings to arise. Allow another minute to pass as you experience this.

4. With your hands still in the self-hugging gesture, repeat the following phrase in a gentle whisper to yourself about ten times. Pause between each statement to feel your hands and your heartbeat.

I am calmly and fully alive in the present moment of my life. My heart and my mind are one.

5. Now take your hands from your chest and bring them to cover your closed eyes, gently palming your face. Experience the darkness, and slowly whisper the same statement to yourself ten times.

I am calmly and fully alive in the present moment of my life. My heart and my mind are one.

6. Finish the exercise by placing your hands on your lap.

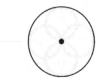

Presence Exercise 2: Standing

Sit on a chair so your back is straight but also relaxed. Make sure your feet are solidly placed on the floor and that you have room to stand. Depending on your strength and the health of your back, you may need a chair with armrests so you can use them to stand when the exercise requires you to do so. I recommend you also remove your shoes. Take a few minutes to get quiet. Follow these steps in a paced way.

1. Notice the sensation of your feet in touch with the ground. Feel, as much as possible, the full bottoms of both your feet touching the ground. Breathe into your feet. (As you inhale, imagine you direct the breath so it moves down from your belly, through your legs, and

into the bottom of your feet.) Take a minute of breathing to connect with the ground or earth beneath your feet.

2. Now, notice the intention to stand up. Introduce the thought, "I am going to stand up." Just be with that thought for a moment, and notice what happens to your attention. Notice if and how the attention moves from or stays with the feet. Notice if your body shifts in any way.

3. Now, prepare to move slowly and then go ahead and stand up as slowly but as safely as possible. Use the armrests if you need to. As you do so, notice where the center of gravity is as you move. You may have a sensation in your belly or between the waistline and belly.

4. As you stand, again, be aware of your feet on the ground. Take a moment to breathe so that your attention again drops down to the sensation of your feet on the ground.

5. Now, notice the intention to sit down. Introduce the thought, "I am going to sit down." Just be with that thought for a moment, and notice what happens to your attention. Notice if and how the attention moves from or stays with the feet. Notice if your body shifts in any way.

6. Now, prepare to move slowly and then go ahead and sit down as slowly but as safely as possible. As you do so, notice where the center of gravity is as you move. You may have a sensation in your belly or between your waistline and your belly.

7. Continue this exercise for a few more rounds. Notice, as you do, how you can direct your attention so that all your movements are coming from a center of gravity in your belly. You can speak this statement aloud as you formulate your intention to move, move, and then stand or sit:

I am deeply centered in my body, in touch with my inner core.

Presence Exercise 3: Quotation Reflection

After taking a few minutes to get quiet, centered, and in a contemplative mood, please reflect on each of these quotations one at a time.

"What day is it?"
"It's today," squeaked Piglet.
"My favorite day," said Pooh.

~A. A. MILNE (ENGLISH AUTHOR)

All that is important is this one moment in movement.
Make the moment important, vital, and worth living.
Do not let it slip away unnoticed and unused.

~MARTHA GRAHAM (AMERICAN MODERN DANCER
AND CHOREOGRAPHER)

The only time we suffer is when we believe a
thought that argues with what is. When the mind
is perfectly clear, "What is" is what we want.

~BYRON KATIE (AMERICAN AUTHOR)

If you were conscious, that is to say totally present
in the Now, all negativity would dissolve almost
instantly. It could not survive your presence.

~ECKHART TOLLE (GERMAN-BORN SPIRITUAL TEACHER)

I say to myself that I shall try to make my life like an open fireplace, so that people may be warmed and cheered by it and so go out themselves to warm and cheer.

~GEORGE MATTHEW ADAMS (AMERICAN NEWSPAPER COLUMNIST)

Being fully present isn't something that happens once and then you achieved it; it's being awake to the ebb and flow and movement and creation of life; being alive to the process of life itself. That also has its softness.

~PEMA CHÖDRÖN (AMERICAN TIBETAN BUDDHIST)

The Christian mystic Hildegard wrote, "God hugs you. You are encircled by the arms of the mystery of God." I have always loved those words, and I believe it is solitude, most of all, that brings us into this circle of presence. But be forewarned: Solitude is no dainty hug.

~SUE MONK KIDD (AMERICAN AUTHOR)

Presence Exercise 4:
Quotation Questions for Journaling or Discussion

1. Which of the above quotations spoke to you the most?

2. Which one reminded you of any current challenge you have to be more present, to "suit up and show up" to your life today, right now?

3. Reflecting on your answers, what do you notice within your body or emotions that might be holding you back from being "all in"?

4. What other quotations, stories, or examples from your own life teach you to be more present?

5. What are the gifts of Presence?

6. What, if any, steps do you want to take to remind yourself about Presence?

Presence Exercise 5: Self-Assessment

There are two sections to this assessment. For both sections, you will rate each statement on a five-point scale from "Rarely true about me" to "Often true about me." The first section lists statements that are worded in a positive direction and indicate more Presence. The second section lists statements worded in a less positive direction. Both sections are important. As you make your selections, make sure you note the rating value (1 to 5 or 5 to 1) and that the values are different for each section.

This statement is true ...	Rarely	Some-times	In Between	Usually	Often
1. I am in touch with my purpose in life.	1	2	3	4	5
2. I am centered in the present moment.	1	2	3	4	5
3. It is easy for me to bring my full attention to things.	1	2	3	4	5

This statement is true ...	Rarely	Some-times	In Between	Usually	Often
4. I always give 100% of my attention in safety-sensitive situations (like driving an automobile).	1	2	3	4	5
5. I feel a strong sense of vitality or aliveness.	1	2	3	4	5
6. I get enough nutrition, exercise, rest, and sleep to have great energy throughout the day.	1	2	3	4	5
7. I cherish each moment of my life.	1	2	3	4	5
8. I enjoy noticing the details, sights, and sounds in my environment.	1	2	3	4	5
9. I easily lose myself in an activity (such a reading, walking, a hobby, or a creative project).	1	2	3	4	5
10. Life feels very real to me.	1	2	3	4	5
11. I get easily stressed.	5	4	3	2	1
12. Change bothers me.	5	4	3	2	1
13. Conditions limit me from fully participating in life.	5	4	3	2	1
14. I am easily distracted by unhelpful activities.	5	4	3	2	1
15. I zone out or feel foggy.	5	4	3	2	1

This statement is true …	Rarely	Some-times	In Between	Usually	Often
16. It is difficult for me to focus.	5	4	3	2	1
17. I feel absent from or not fully engaged in my life.	5	4	3	2	1
18. I spend too much time on my cell phone or the internet.	5	4	3	2	1
19. I struggle with finding time for inner warmth or calm.	5	4	3	2	1
20. I am busy or just have too many things to do.	5	4	3	2	1

After you have completed rating all twenty items, please total your scores. The total score you could receive ranges from 20 to 100. The score you receive can change from time to time, so please check back and rate yourself on these items as often as you would like. This is not a test designed to pigeonhole you in a particular personality "type" or to help you diagnose any problem you might have. Instead, treat it as an opportunity to reflect on how much right now, in this moment, you have access to this attitude of Presence. Just notice what score you have today. Be present to that. Fully.

Presence Exercise 6:
Self-Assessment Questions for Journaling or Discussion

1. What are your internal and emotional reactions to the score you received?

2. Do you notice more of a tendency to quickly react to the score or more of a tendency to just sit with and process the meaning of the score?

3. Which of the twenty statements caused you most to think, "This is me," or really captured your current level of Presence? Explain why.

4. Which one reminded you of any current challenge you have with living in the moment, getting yourself free of distraction, and being fully present to yourself and the world around you?

5. Reflecting on your answers, what do you notice about your internal chatter, being distracted by thoughts of the past or future, or your inability to stay focused and present?

6. What are your core strengths of Presence?

7. What appears to be getting in the way of Presence?

8. What, if any, steps do you want to take to remind yourself about Presence?

REFLECTION

In graduate school, I worked as a part-time educator for the National Safety Training Institute (NSTI), teaching Saturday courses on both beginner's defensive driving and also a court-required course for those who were ticketed for driving while intoxicated (DWI) and repeat traffic offenders. The latter included drivers with many—sometimes a half-dozen—speeding tickets. Ironically, at the time, I myself had barely driven a car and had never owned a car. While I relied on public transportation, I had been involved in several minor car accidents: as a youth due to my father's road rage and as a teenager due to drug use by my friends behind the wheel. I had been to the hospital with only minor injuries. So I had some experience upon which to draw when teaching the course. I taught the course about two or three dozen times, often with between 25 to 40 participants from all walks of life in attendance.

The NSTI model was based on making decisions while driving that followed one's values. The vast majority of students who came to the class were there to receive a certificate of attendance as required by insurance or by the court. Needless to say, values were not top of mind. At some point, while teaching the first part of the course, I began focusing on one single question that seemed to engage most everyone: "Have you ever had a wake-up call in your life, where something happened, usually outside of your control, that required you to really look at your values in life?" If participants couldn't relate, I would add: "This could be an example of an accident, death, loss, failure."

Typically, there were two or three people who would be willing to speak up, usually somewhat older than others in the class. They shared about a fire burning their home down, a family member killed in a car accident, flunking out of school, and other tragedies. Often, when they shared, other students would listen with undivided attention. The Presence in the room was palpable. At the time, I often had the thought that I wished I could bottle up that level of attention and keep using it for the rest of the day. Much of the remainder of the class was on the dry mechanics of defensive driving. I saw that my job was to keep connecting the decision to *be present while driving* to the student's values of life, safety, and care for others.

That was in the basic class, which touched the surface of values. The DWI and repeat offenders' class was a different and more entertaining story. These were smaller classes and often had at least one of the following types of individuals: someone in the legal professions (lawyer or judge), an entertainer, or someone with an addiction. One story I will never forget is when a student shared how they woke up in a field with a cow licking their face. This was in the morning, and the field was hundreds of miles away from their home, in another state entirely. They never knew how they got there. In another story, the motorcyclist proudly shared how he was able to outmaneuver the police on the interstate for ten miles before getting caught.

Teaching the NSTI course was not my first real-world experience with Presence, but it was the most important. I learned that despite the potential lethality of the automobile, most people take their attention and Presence for granted and go "on automatic" while driving. I discovered that it was possible, through a brief educational course, to change this attitude for many (although, admittedly, not all). I figured out that addiction and positions of power—as in the case of the lawyers and judges— can lead to a sense of invulnerability that diminishes Presence. The law is there to protect us from those who are not present. Most of all, I learned that human beings might need a wake-up call to become more present in their lives and treat them with care and responsibility.

My actual real-world introduction to, and lesson about, Presence had come more than ten years earlier when, as a fifteen-year-old, I had a brief job working as a "grease monkey" at a gas station. (They now call them "lube experts.") Everyone there knew I did not have a driver's license when they hired me. I also told them I had never driven before and that I would prefer to work only under the cars and not in them. Still, one day they asked me to back a van out of the driveway so they could position another car for lubing. Again, I explained that I did not know how. Nevertheless, I found myself doing it. Of course, I got fired that day after scraping the side of the van. The lesson? I learned that I had to trust my own gut as to whether I am up to being present to any task or challenge before me. I can use, but not solely rely on, the guidance and input of others. Ultimately, the moment where we are confronted with safety risk may be the best teacher of Presence. And sometimes, Presence means saying an emphatic "No!"

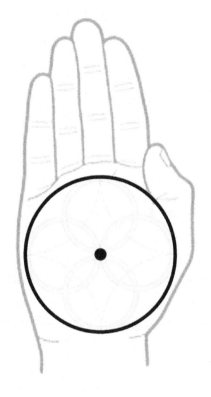

All is Presence

CHAPTER 5

Flow

Ode to Flow

Everyday something transforms.

Absorb yourself, leap into, and taste it.
Until the next cycle.
Then start again.

Ever look forward to BE with
The Tao, the River, the Endless Stream.

Then, just adore it all.
Really, that
is all
you need
to ever do.

again and again and again …

~J.B.

There has been a significant amount of research on flow following the pioneering work of Mihalyi Csikszentmihalyi and measurement studies by Susan Jackson and colleagues. Their conception of flow informs the approach taken here. As a Soulful Capacity, Flow must be considered and applied in the broadest sense possible. In this happening life, your greatest performance will likely be how well you *intend* to use, *actively* use, and *have used* the time you have been given. Here is how Csikszentmihalyi defines Flow:

> *A state in which people are so involved in an activity that nothing else seems to matter; the experience is so enjoyable that people will continue to do it even at great cost, for the sheer sake of doing it (Csikszentmihalyi, from Flow: The Psychology of Optimal Experience, 1990, page 4).*

There are two important insights drawn from this work. First, that people can cultivate the ability to access this Flow state on an ongoing basis. Such people have an *autotelic* personality (from *auto* for self and *telos* for end or purpose). This means they tend to approach life and its tasks as having an end or purpose in themselves. They are both intrinsically motivated by and actively absorbed in the Flow of life, rarely bored, and see stress as a transforming challenge rather than an obstacle. Second, there are eight different features to the experience of Flow. The first seven include: having a chance to complete the task; concentrating on what we are doing; having clear goals along the path; getting immediate feedback from our actions; merging our actions with awareness to the exclusion of worries and distractions; having a sense of control; and regarding the activity as having an inherent purpose as an end in itself.

The eighth feature relates directly to time as described by Csikszentmihalyi. He explains that our sense of duration of time is altered; hours pass by in minutes, and minutes can stretch out to seem like hours. This is the manifestation of "time flies when you are having fun." Many studies on Flow assess creativity, play, leisure activities, and idle time. In one study of elderly people, those who had higher levels of psychological function (less depression, feeling younger than one's age) were more likely to feel that "time flies," whereas institutionalized elders felt time moved more slowly.

This last finding speaks to the purpose of this book and your soulful capacity at any stage of life, young or old. In an earlier section in Book 1 of QfP (The Time Adjustment Protocol), readers are asked to complete an exercise where they draw the timeline of their life on a sheet of paper. Imagine that the timeline represents this entire journey of life, with various milestones. Again, you are an explorer on a mission to discover treasure. Based on our understanding of different stages of life from Erik Erikson, here are the tasks and goals along the path of life:

1. Trusting that the world is a safe place, where there is enough consistency and predictability to learn what we need to do and carry out all other tasks. Goals: Feeling cared for and held by others or one's family/tribe; a sense of hope, optimism, trust.

2. Feeling independence and a sense of control and autonomy over one's own actions. Goals: Feeling confidence and self-efficacy; the ability to have a sense of completion; the ability to play.

3. Initiating and planning activities, taking opportunities to shape one's own environment, and questing and exploring. Goals: Feeling a sense of purpose, that one's actions may have some recognized value in the world.

4. Developing a sense of competency, industry, or mastery; a sense of pride that one's accomplishments are valued by peers. Goals: Feeling competent and fully confident that others benefit from one's skills.

5. Developing a sense of identity and role clarity regarding one's place in society. Goals: Feeling that one can commit oneself to others, that one can adapt to changing opinions and others' differences while maintaining a core sense of identity.

6. Forming intimate, close, and loving relationships with other people; a sense that one can share inner thoughts and feelings. Goals: Feeling love in an ongoing way that protects against feelings of isolation, loneliness, alienation, or depression.

7. Making one's mark in the world by creating and nurturing things that will outlast one's own lifetime. Goals: Feeling a sense of having

been productive, of having given back to society, that one has been a caring person.

8. Coming to terms with and accepting one's entire life story to have a sense of coherence and wholeness. Goals: Feeling a sense of wisdom, the ability to look back on life with a sense of completeness, wholeness, and without any fear of death.

As you reflect on the wide expanse of these challenges or tasks, realize that they can all fit within the features of Flow. Not only may your life have clear tasks and goals, but you may—God willing—have the chance to concentrate on and fulfill them. At the very least, you can focus on and get completely absorbed in your current life task so that it becomes an end in itself. That would be this happening life!

Other Qualities of Flow

We also experience Flow when we can get absorbed with things, when we can follow our own joyful impulses to do something for the sake of doing it, when we can relish and delight in the moment, and when we maintain a positive outlook despite life's challenges. Even more, we can use challenges to our advantage. My favorite quote about Flow captures this perfectly:

> *Of all the virtues we can learn no trait is more*
> *useful, more essential to survival, and more likely*
> *to improve the quality of life than the ability to*
> *transform adversity into an enjoyable challenge.*

~M. CSIKSZENTMIHALYI (HUNGARIAN-AMERICAN PSYCHOLOGIST)

Flow includes aspects of both Acceptance and Presence. It is different from them in that the sequential Flow of time becomes more present or salient. Acceptance means *allowing* what is; Presence means *being fully with* what is; Flow means a sense of *becoming or merging with what is just about to unfold* in a more moment-to-moment and give-and-take with what unfolds. The distinctions between Acceptance, Presence, and Flow are most vivid during life's transitions.

REFLECTION

In my own life, I can *accept* that my wife wants to spend more time with our grandchildren, as I want the same and for her to be happy. But accepting is different from being *present* to her desire to engage in a conversation to coordinate our schedules and make specific plans. Often, I have other work tasks and personal needs (distractions) that I wish to attend to. Only when I let go of my own needs am I able to be in *Flow* with her. We collaborate about plans that result in mutual satisfaction as we move together into spaces with our grandchildren. And, the rewards from flowing with the family and the twists and turns of a child's attention are some of the greatest treasures of life.

Contemplation (Q*f*P 2-4): Flow

Flow Exercise 1:
Flowing Through the Stages of Life, a Reflection

This first exercise asks you to: (1) look at the big picture of life and the eight developmental tasks outlined by Erik Erikson; (2) reflect on which of the challenges are most present in your life right now; (3) identify how much you are able to *flow with, flow through,* and *flow positively* (learn, grow, and mature) because of these challenges; and (4) utilize all the exercises (affirmations and quotations) in this entire section on Soulful Capacities to gather confidence for the task.

What Are the Challenges? First, using the brief survey below, indicate how much each of the eight areas is a life challenge for you right now.

What Is the Greatest Challenge? Second, select the one or two that are the most challenging right now.

What Feature of Flow Can You Access? Third, consider which features of Flow you already have that will allow you to address the challenge. For now, just select one thing you can do.

EIGHT FEATURES OF FLOW

1. I seize any chance to meet the challenge

2. I fully concentrate on the task at hand

3. I seek immediate feedback on how well I am doing

4. I remove distractions and worries to fully immerse myself

5. I set and follow clear goals to meet the challenge

6. I build up my confidence, sense of control, and efficacy

7. The challenge is inherently meaningful, full of purpose

8. I enjoy letting things unfold in the process of meeting the challenge

---

Developmental Challenges	(Step 1) How much of a challenge?			(Step 2) Select your top challenge	(Step 3) How can you address it?
	Not at all	Some-what	Definitely		See Eight Features of Flow
Difficulty trusting what is happening in my life.				☐	
Lacking a sense of independence, control, or autonomy.				☐	
Unable to get things started, make a change, initiate a project, or explore an opportunity that could help me.				☐	
Feeling like a failure, not feeling good at what I do, or feeling that others do not value my contributions.				☐	
Feeling lost, uncertain of my direction, identity, or real place in the world.				☐	
Unable to form intimate, close relationships; unable to share who I am; feeling lonely or isolated.				☐	
Lacking a sense that I have yet to create or nurture something that will be of lasting value after I die.				☐	
Unable to accept the story of my life as a whole, lacking a sense of wholeness or completion.				☐	

Flow Exercise 2: Quotation Reflection

After taking a few minutes to get quiet, centered, and in a contemplative mood, please reflect on each of these quotations one at a time.

Those who flow as life flows know they need no other force.

~LAO TZU (TAOIST SAGE)

The problem with life is that it flows and is not graspable.
The beauty of life is that it runs and does not stop.

~JOAN CHITTISTER (AMERICAN THEOLOGIAN)

The only way to make sense out of change is to
plunge into it, move with it, and join the dance.

~ALAN WILSON WATTS
(ENGLISH AUTHOR AND PHILOSOPHER)

In a state of grace, the soul is like a well of limpid water,
from which flow only streams of clearest crystal.

~SAINT TERESA OF AVILA
(16ᵀᴴ CENTURY SPANISH MYSTIC)

Faith is the opening of all sides and every
level of one's life in the Divine in-flow.

~MARTIN LUTHER KING, JR.
(AMERICAN BAPTIST MINISTER AND ACTIVIST)

*Therefore, we will not fear, though the earth gives way
and the mountains fall into the heart of the sea, though
its waters roar and foam and the mountains quake with
their surging; There is a river whose streams make glad the
city of God, the holy place where the Most High dwells.*

~PSALM 46:2-4 (NIV)

Flow Exercise 3:
Quotation Questions for Journaling or Discussion

1. Which of the above quotations spoke to you the most?

2. Which one reminded you of any current challenge you have to being more in Flow with life, to touch into that soulful part of you that can Flow right now?

3. Reflecting on your answers, what do you notice about any area of your life where you could make more efforts to rise to the challenge and go with the Flow?

4. What other quotations, stories, or examples from your own life teach you about being more flowing?

5. What are the gifts of Flow?

6. What, if any, steps do you want to take to remind yourself about Flow?

Flow Exercise 4: Self-Assessment

There are two sections to this assessment. For both sections, you will rate each statement on a five-point scale from "Rarely true about me" to "Often true about me." The first section lists statements that are worded in a positive direction and indicate more capacity for Flow. The second lists statements worded in a less positive direction. Both sections are important. As you make your selections, make sure you note the rating value (1 to 5 or 5 to 1) and that the values are different for each section.

This statement is true …	Rarely	Some-times	In Between	Usually	Often
1. I easily flow with change.	1	2	3	4	5
2. I am competent enough to meet demanding situations.	1	2	3	4	5
3. I get so absorbed in tasks that time disappears.	1	2	3	4	5
4. I feel in control of the events unfolding in my life.	1	2	3	4	5
5. I easily transition into different activities in my life.	1	2	3	4	5
6. I enjoy doing things spontaneously and without having to think.	1	2	3	4	5

This statement is true …	Rarely	Some-times	In Between	Usually	Often
7. I am good at savoring simple things.	1	2	3	4	5
8. While working or on a project, I clearly know how well things are progressing.	1	2	3	4	5
9. I have a strong sense of what I want to do.	1	2	3	4	5
10. I enjoy most of my daily tasks just for the sake of doing them.	1	2	3	4	5
11. My life is in disarray or disordered.	5	4	3	2	1
12. It is difficult for me to be spontaneous.	5	4	3	2	1
13. My life is more mechanical than in an easy flow.	5	4	3	2	1
14. I wish I could be more optimistic.	5	4	3	2	1
15. I don't have a hobby or pastime that I really lose myself in.	5	4	3	2	1
16. Time seems to drag.	5	4	3	2	1
17. I don't take time to just sit back and enjoy life.	5	4	3	2	1
18. I do not feel invigorated by a challenge.	5	4	3	2	1
19. My life is boring.	5	4	3	2	1
20. I wish I had time to explore new things.	5	4	3	2	1

After you have completed rating all twenty items, please total your scores. The total score you could receive ranges from 20 to 100. The score you receive can change from time to time, so please check back and rate yourself on these items as often as you would like. This is not a test designed to pigeonhole you in a particular personality "type" or to help you diagnose any problem you might have. Instead, treat it as an opportunity to reflect on how much, right now in this moment, you have access to this attitude of Flow. For this reason, I suggest you refrain from comparing your score with others or judging yourself in any way. That would defeat the purpose of the exercise. Just notice what score you have today. How much—right now—can you access the attitude of Flow? How can you "flow" with the information you have as a result of the ratings you made?

Flow Exercise 5:
Self-Assessment Questions for Journaling or Discussion

1. What are your internal and emotional reactions to the score you received?

2. Do you notice more of a tendency to analyze and compartmentalize your score or more of a tendency to be excited about how you can grow from the feedback?

3. Which of the twenty statements caused you most to think "This is me," or really captured your current level of Flow? Explain why.

4. Which one reminded you of any current challenge you have with practicing the art of flowing, of just getting absorbed in your life, being spontaneous, savoring, or optimistic?

5. Reflecting on your answers, what do you notice about your internal chatter? How can you see yourself moving away or toward Flow?

6. What are your core strengths of Flow?

7. What appears to be getting in the way of Flow?

8. What, if any, steps do you want to take to remind yourself about Flow?

REFLECTION

My wife and I dated for two years, broke up, and then nine years later, we got married. I had helped care for her two toddler sons in our first go-round, and we shared many joyful times together. However, I left because I was too insecure to handle the responsibilities of forging a new career while managing the dynamics of what I experienced as a difficult stepfamily situation. When I returned, the boys were on the cusp of adolescence. I walked into a situation similar to the one I had left, but, I hoped, with more wisdom to show from a few more years on the planet.

Two significant lessons stand out during the transition time into the new stepfamily situation. They are completely due to the patience of my wife, her ability to Flow, and her ability to teach me something about Flow. In the first experience, I remember all four of us standing outside our black Toyota station wagon. We were discussing what we were going to do that day, or do in the next hour, or even the next moment. I had no clue what was happening—which was a regular occurrence. One of my stepsons emphatically stated that our plans were diametrically opposed to the needs of the other stepson. They were arguing, laughing, and screaming all at the same time. Apparently, whatever plans I had made with my wife were no longer a priority.

My job was to just relax and be present. I distinctly remember starting to react, moving into the first stages of my "storming off" routine. My wife, seeing what was happening, grabbed me by the shoulders with a firm but calm Presence. She looked deeply into my eyes with her own beautiful, light emerald-green eyes and repeated several times, in a very calm voice, "Flow." It worked. In that moment, I felt safe, I was seen, I could handle the situation, and time sort of stood still. The kids were still acting out, and my wife continued to manage the chaos. It seems that my own newly found calm may have had some influence on the situation.

The second experience occurred around the same time and pointed to trust and safety as conditions for Flow (see Exercise 1 on page 69). We were at one of the boys' first soccer games after my return to the family. The other side of the family was there: the boys' father, wife, and grandparents. I believed that I had no real place in the family system, riddled as I was with self-doubt about my role as a stepfather. My wife took me by the hand and walked with me up and down the perimeter of the 100-yard athletic field. As we walked, I could see the figures of my stepsons on the field, the other family members, and everyone else. Their impressions on my eyes got larger and then smaller as we walked toward or away from them. With her hand in mine, I felt worries diminish. I could see myself flowing within the bigger picture of our life together, and I had some sense of manageability and control.

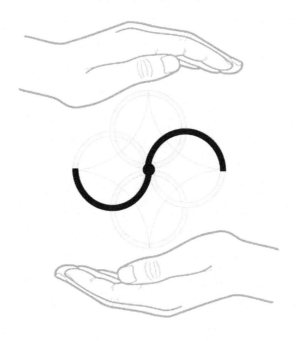

All is Flow

CHAPTER 6

Synchronicity

Ode to Synchronicity

Everyday something connects, vibrates at
the same frequency of something else.

That would be you there.
That is you there.

Connecting. Tuning In. Jiving.
Frolicking.
Effortlessly, your life shows up to itself.

~J.B.

More than 100 billion galaxies sprawl across the vast universe. In a fanciful, numerical coincidence, more than 100 billion human beings have ever been born on the planet. Our human life, with our inherent capacity to be conscious of the universe, is one of the most meaningful occurrences we may ever know. Most of us have an inkling that we are not here by mere chance. We wonder, "Why was I born at this particular time in history?"

Indeed, these are wonders: the very presence of our Planet Earth, its capacity to breed all of life, and the human race. Our galaxy, our planet, the human species, or our particular life cannot be a simple happenstance, an incident of chance. Perhaps, through the farthest future of science, the evolution of humanity and also human consciousness, we will unveil the meaning of it all. We will discern a pattern that connects it all together.

We often don't reflect on these matters. It is enough to just work on accepting and being present to what is happening in our lives now. And yet, from time to time, we have an experience that intrudes into our plans, our schedules and routines, and makes us wonder. Something unexpected and unplanned happens *at the same time* as our being there. We feel a resonance, a connection; something momentous, poignant, meaningful; and it apparently required no direct effort on our part.

Frederic and Mary Ann Brussat, authors of *Spiritual Rx: Prescriptions for Living a Meaningful Life*, write about Synchronicity as a topic on their website, Spirituality and Practice.

> *All of us have experienced magic moments of synchronicity: the anticipation of a call seconds before the phone rings, a chance meeting with an old friend who has just the advice we need, or a feeling of connection with a loved one miles away just as s/he is dying. Such happenings signal the hidden meanings in the universe which call us to be as attentive as poets and as curious as detectives looking for clues (Frederic and Mary Ann Brussat, from www.spiritualityandpractice.com (topic of synchronicity).*

Of the Soulful Capacities, Synchronicity is the most tied to occasions, events, and our search for meaning. The experience can be creative, poetic, and almost magical. We not only detect coincidences, we are emotionally altered by them. For many people, the emotion itself is so uncommon or difficult to grasp through logic that we say, "That was weird!" And they never give it a second thought. Alternately, when it comes to falling in love, or feeling that you have met the right person at the right time, the feeling of fit or alignment is more uplifting and surprisingly familiar.

In moving from Acceptance to Presence to Flow, we get more in touch with our bodies, our sensations, and the world around us. We become more fully embodied in the world. We arrive in our life. We grow less and less attached to clock-time and the passing of time. We acclimate more and more to the greater dance of cosmic forces (described fully in *QfP Book 1*). Synchronicity is entirely different, almost like a quantum jump. Our souls attune to a whole different quality of time, one that takes us more fully into the forces themselves. Reflect on both the technical definition (from www.definitions.net) and a quote adapted from the 2001 movie *Serendipity*.

synchronicity *noun*
The experience of two or more events that are apparently causally unrelated or unlikely to occur together by chance, yet are experienced as occurring together in a meaningful manner.

Life is not merely a series of meaningless accidents or coincidences. … But rather, it is a tapestry of acts that culminate in an exquisite, sublime plan.

~FROM THE 2001 MOVIE *SERENDIPITY*
(DIRECTED BY PETER CHELSOM)

Elements of Synchronicity

These two excerpts suggest four main elements to Synchronicity. These are simultaneity, the appearance of chance, meaningfulness, and an intimacy between our interior timing and the exterior timing of the world.

+ **Simultaneity**: when at least two things co-occur simultaneously— moments, occasions, a time in our life.

+ **Appearance of Chance**: this co-occurrence *seems* to be just a chance happening, a coincidence, an accident.

+ **Meaningfulness**: despite appearances, the co-occurrence is filled with meaning, as though it were part of a plan we cannot fathom. It was Our Fate, Kismet, destined to happen. (In fact, research on meaningful coincidences suggests that those who have them tend not to believe they are the result of chance.)

✦ **Interior/Exterior Merger**: two arms embrace Synchronicity. The exterior world (*exteriority*) *breaks into* the ordinary, while a soulful stirring (*intrapsychic*) *fills us up with* some knowing, a sense that we are onto something or something special is happening.

These same four elements parallel nearly every spiritual or religious guidance in the quest for the soul. Teachers call us to (1) emerge from this *veil* of appearances, (2) cut through the *chaos* and its play of chance, (3) move on to find your destiny, and (4) let the spirit in, allow God to enter your life, or abandon yourself.

Synchronicity as a Skill

With the Soulful Capacity of Synchronicity, this quest is always occurring. It can always be fulfilled in this moment. We need not wait for science and the future evolution of humanity to show us the truth. We each have the capacity to touch into this place.

> *Yesterday they called it coincidence. Today it's synchronicity. Tomorrow they'll call it skill.*
>
> ~ANTERO ALLI (ASTROLOGER, AUTHOR, AND UNDERGROUND FILMMAKER)

A number of authors claim that we can develop this capacity for synchronicity or serendipity. There are several things to note about this skill. First, that just because we do not see Synchronicity happening at the time does not mean that it is not happening. Second, while not everything *appears* synchronistic, it is possible that *at some level, everything* is a Synchronicity. Third, keep in mind that not all synchronicities are good or fortunate. One study suggests positive coincidences are more frequently reported, and people find more meaning during positive rather than negative events. However, coincidences may be related as much to events that are negative (injury, illness, death, divorce, stress) as to positive (marriage, birth of a child, promotion, vacation). Finally, mere coincidence, serendipity, and Synchronicity are related but different.

> *Serendipity is when something good accidentally happens. For instance, we may need cash to pay for unexpected vet bills and find some in our jacket pocket that we've just put on.*
>
> *Synchronicity, on the other hand, is not just a single experience of good fortune.* **Synchronicity is a string of events that seem to be highly symbolic and meaningful in nature.**
>
> *If serendipity is like the bread crumb, synchronicity is the trail that leads us toward a new destination. Many people see synchronicity as a lesson, affirmation, or message from Life.*
>
> *One example of synchronicity is hearing the same name over and over again (in books, on TV, on number plates, in dreams) and later discovering that the name is a suburb where you finally find your dream home (Aletheia Luna, 2021, from https://lonerwolf.com/synchronicity/).*

I believe that as we learn to develop serendipity, we also can develop Synchronicity. Below is a quick summary of some claims about the skill of Synchronicity, in terms of how I have adapted and interpreted them for this book. The elements are derived from the work of Carl Jung, Robert H. Hopcke, Sanda Erdelez, Mateo Sol, Roderick Main, and others.

Elements in the Skill of Synchronicity

1. **Believe in yourself as a "serendipiter" or Synchronicity detective.** Research suggests that you can be an explorer or detective who looks for clues or signs for serendipity. Pek van Andel, known as a *serendipitologist*, writes, "Serendipity is the art of making an unsought finding." You have a special set of antennae for seeing

the "pattern that connects" things in nature. Our understanding of these antennae is informed by research in information science on browsing and search behaviors among those using a library or the internet. Being a serendipiter requires having some initial spark or interest in the subject matter, having an intention to learn more about it, and being willing to browse both related and unrelated subject matter in a way that is not too goal-oriented. It is like being willing to take a side road on the journey (see the Treasure of "Spontaneity" in Book 5 of QfP).

2. **Reframe the "sign" as a symbol.** The German philosopher Ernst Cassirer wrote in his 1944 *An Essay on Man*, "A sign is part of the physical world of being, a symbol is part of the human world of meaning." As noted above, Synchronicity is not just mental. It is also inspirational and emotional. It brings about great meaning. Similarly, if a serendipiter looked for signs only as a prompt to take another step, to do something, to uncover some source information, or to have an aha moment, they might miss the *symbolic* aspect of the experience and its greater importance to their spiritual journey. Instead of being simply a piece of information, the event must be seen as providence, a revelation, an Opening, a Transcendence. We are looking not only *for* the sign but also for *how* it is spiritually nourishing. It nourishes our entire life or, at least, a particular turn in the unfolding of our destiny.

3. **Go with your instincts; have trust and humility.** Synchronistic experiences may not happen because we will them to. For example, just because you want to find the perfect marriage partner does not mean you will cross their path. Instead, it is important to trust life and allow things to unfold while having a humble attitude. At the same time, it helps to go with your instincts. If you have an inkling or intuition that tells you to take the side road, follow your gut.

4. **Pray and use visioning practices.** By praying, setting intentions, doing certain meditation practices, or repeating affirmations, it is

possible to create a mental attitude whereby we become more open to synchronistic events.

5. **See wholeness.** We each can see wholeness or sense how things fit together. Often, however, when synchronistic events or occasions occur, we may not recognize them *at the time*. We do not, *right then*, intuitively place or frame how the event fits into the wholeness of our lives. Instead, we make sense of it only afterward and through our capacity for wholeness.

6. **Let go of what you think is so.** Because of our current limited view or ego, we may not ask for or want the event. We may even resist it. Often, we need to take seriously what is being presented in our lives. There is something *within the event* that is calling us to let go of something, and we may not realize it until we let go.

7. **Cultivate a capacity for experiencing deep emotion.** Synchronicity is rarely just a mental perception or recognition of coincidence. It awakens, evokes, touches, or stirs something within us at a deep emotional level: awe, amazement, joy. It is as though somewhere in the universe, there was a messenger who cared about your evolution so much that they conspired with "everyday" reality to awaken you with deep emotion. That is, the situation was not a coincidence, but rather, it was a feeling that arrived in your soul, awakening you to recognize it in the form of a coincidence. It was always there; you just had to feel it.

8. **Allow the story to come forth.** We cannot anticipate or predict a synchronistic event. It either happens during a life transition, or it marks and defines the transition in our life story. That is, our stories—how we knit together and then share what has happened to us—reveal a Synchronicity. When we pause to reflect on how "that time" was a momentous transition, we realize how events aligned to make the transition happen. Sometimes, it is only when we start sharing the story that we realize the alignment.

Contemplation (QfP 2-5): Synchronicity

Synchronicity Exercise 1: Quotation Reflection

After taking a few minutes to get quiet, centered, and in a contemplative mood, please reflect on each of these quotations one at a time.

1. *Chance favors the prepared mind.*

   ~LOUIS PASTEUR (19TH CENTURY FRENCH CHEMIST)

2. *What you seek is seeking you.*

   ~JALALUDDIN MUHAMMAD RUMI (SUFI POET, MYSTIC)

3. *Tragedies, joys, triumphs, failures, frustrations,*
   crises … behind every development, small and
   large, is something else, something meaningful,
   a hidden gift, that if received with grace and used
   with reverence, invites me a step higher on my journey.

   ~CAROL LYNN PEARSON
   (AMERICAN POET AND AUTHOR)

4. *When I pray, coincidences start to happen.*
   When I don't pray, they don't happen.

   ~ARCHBISHOP WILLIAM TEMPLE
   (ENGLISH ANGLICAN PRIEST)

5. *To see a World in a Grain of Sand, And a Heaven in a Wild Flower, Hold Infinity in the palm of your hand, And Eternity in an hour.*

~WILLIAM BLAKE
(18TH CENTURY ENGLISH POET AND VISIONARY)

6. *No coincidence, no story.*

~LISA SEE (AMERICAN AUTHOR)

7. *The universe is always speaking to us ... Sending us little messages, causing coincidences and serendipities, reminding us to stop, to look around, to believe in something else, something more.*

~NANCY THAYER (AMERICAN NOVELIST)

Synchronicity Exercise 2:
Quotation Items for Journaling or Discussion

1. First and foremost, describe any experiences you have had—whether a simple coincidence, a serendipity, or a deep life-changing Synchronicity.

2. Approach this exercise differently from the previous quotation exercises. First, note which of the above quotations spoke to you the most. Next, notice that the quotations are numbered from 1 to 7. Rank the remaining quotations in order from your most favorite

to your least favorite. After you have done so, pause before reading the next item.

3. As you review your rank ordering, take a look at your *least* preferred quotation. First, explain why it is your least preferred. Next, explain what possible relationship it has with your most preferred.

4. Review your preferences alongside the eight elements of Synchronicity capacity described in this chapter. What connection do you see between your preference and these elements? Is there a particular element that might be your strength, and can you use the quote to inspire you?

Again, the elements are:

a. Believe in yourself as a "serendipiter" or synchronicity detective.

b. Reframe the "sign" as a symbol.

c. Go with your instincts; have trust and humility.

d. Pray and use visioning practices.

e. See wholeness.

f. Let go of what you think is so.

g. Cultivate a capacity for experiencing deep emotion.

h. Allow the story to come forth.

5. What other quotations, stories, or examples from your own life teach you about Synchronicity?

6. What are the gifts of Synchronicity?

7. What, if any, steps do you want to take to remind yourself about Synchronicity?

Synchronicity Exercise 3: Self-Assessment

There are two sections to this assessment. For both sections, you will rate each statement on a five-point scale from "Rarely true about me" to "Often true about me." The first section lists statements that are worded in a positive direction and indicate more capacity for Synchronicity. The second lists statements worded in a less positive direction. Both sections are important. As you make your selections, make sure you note the rating value (1 to 5 or 5 to 1) and that the values are different for the two sections below.

This statement is true …	Rarely	Some- times	In Between	Usually	Often
1. I have serendipitous moments. (For example, I am in the right place at the right time; I think about something I had lost and then turn to find it immediately).	1	2	3	4	5
2. I find myself thinking, "Everything is happening just like it is supposed to be happening."	1	2	3	4	5
3. My life story unfolds in ways that feel like destiny.	1	2	3	4	5
4. I have been spiritually nourished by people I met by accident (such as a stranger or a chance meeting).	1	2	3	4	5

This statement is true …	Rarely	Some-times	In Between	Usually	Often
5. I see the deeper meaning of events.	1	2	3	4	5
6. There have been moments in my life where everything came together in a meaningful way.	1	2	3	4	5
7. I have faith in my own intuition.	1	2	3	4	5
8. I have read books or seen movies with events that are identical to parts of my life story.	1	2	3	4	5
9. Certain events hold hidden gifts and were meant to happen.	1	2	3	4	5
10. I do practices that leave me open to Synchronicity happening in my life (such as prayer, meditation, and visualizations).	1	2	3	4	5
11. It is hard for me to see the meaning of it all.	5	4	3	2	1
12. I am in complete control of everything that happens in my life.	5	4	3	2	1
13. Powerful or intense emotions are difficult for me.	5	4	3	2	1
14. I am 100% the captain of my own fate.	5	4	3	2	1
15. I am a "what you see is what you get" type of person.	5	4	3	2	1

This statement is true ...	Rarely	Some-times	In Between	Usually	Often
16. Life makes no sense to me.	5	4	3	2	1
17. Negative or painful events have happened to me that have never made any sense.	5	4	3	2	1
18. I don't see much benefit in looking at art or sculpture.	5	4	3	2	1
19. My life decisions are based more on logic and analysis than intuition or going with my gut.	5	4	3	2	1
20. Any so-called "meaningful coincidence" is really just due to chance and mathematical probability.	5	4	3	2	1

Please review the scoring instructions for the previous measures of Soulful Capacities. As before, use your total score as an opportunity to reflect on how much, right now in this moment, you have access to this capacity. Just notice what score you have today. Was there something about it or in any of the items that happen to coincide in a meaningful way with something else that is happening in your life right now?

Synchronicity Exercise 4:
Self-Assessment Questions for Journaling or Discussion

1. What are your internal and emotional reactions to the score you received?

2. What do you make of the differences between the more "positive" items (1 to 10) and the remaining items (11 to 20)? Do you agree or think that the latter items can hurt your chances of Synchronicity? Do they matter at all? If you feel you scored fairly low on the first set of items, can you still have a deep capacity for Synchronicity?

3. An exercise: Which one item from the first set (1 to 10) do you *most* agree with? Which from the second set (11 to 20) do you *most* agree with? Reflect on how these might be related to each other. Copy these two statements onto a Post-it Note™ or paper and tape it to a place that you look at daily (computer monitor, refrigerator door, bathroom mirror, bedside). See if there is "some message" there.

4. What are your core strengths of Synchronicity?

5. What appears to be getting in the way of Synchronicity?

6. What, if any, steps do you want to take to remind yourself about Synchronicity?

REFLECTION

One winter vacation in college, I attended a nine-day silent spiritual retreat. One night early in the retreat, I had a lucid dream. I was visited by what may be best described as a woman spirit guide and lover. Her dark, midnight-blue body was made of starry filaments. At one point, she whispered the words "rod" and "hill" several times over. I woke up feeling I had a real encounter, not a dream.

Shortly after the retreat, I received a call that my mother had died of a heart attack. This was a shock. While she was not in the best of health at the age of forty-four, there was no strong sign that she was at risk. As my father had left, my brother and I were responsible for closing up the apartment and taking care of her belongings. It took a while for me to work through the logistics to return to school.

The whole time while dealing with my mother's passing, I kept thinking about the dream. I had previously seen a Jungian psychologist at the college counseling center and had some idea about working with dream symbols. I thought of Moses with his staff on Mount Sinai. Was the rod the wand of wisdom and the hill a chance to have perspective on life? As I struggled to figure it out, I would share the dream with friends. One friend said, "That may not mean anything; you must know that the new counseling center therapist's name is Rodman Hill."

This news was baffling for two reasons. First, I had not recalled learning about the new therapist. It had been many months since I had seen the previous one. So, I may have had that information, but it was peripheral. Second, the dream was so powerful and vivid that I was convinced it must hold deep, symbolic meaning. It took some time, but I decided to go to Rodman Hill and ask him what he thought of my dream.

Now, Rodman was not a Jungian psychologist. He seemed to have no real interest in symbolism but wanted to find out more about what bothered me and how I was dealing with college. As I recall, I did not really talk much about my mom at the beginning of the session. I was really trying to figure out what Rodman thought about the fact that I had this powerful dream with his name in it.

As the conversation progressed, I talked more and more about my mom. Then, at one point, Rodman asked me, "When did your mom die?" I responded by telling him that I had already told him "during the Christmas break." But then he asked again, "No, I mean, what day did she die?" I thought this was curious, but when I told him, he replied, "My mother died that same day as well." I asked, "You mean she died on that day years ago?" Rodman clarified by saying, "No, she died on the exact same day as your mother." After that, he just shook his head and said he could not help me.

I left that session, never to return to see Rodman. Among the many intuitions I have had about this experience, I know two things most clearly. First, the woman spirit guide was a premonition and encounter more than a dream. The likelihood of her coming to me *before* both deaths could not be explained by chance alone. Second, while I might have explored a relationship with Rodman, I was not inclined or ready to do so at the time. Something inside me knew that the meaning would be revealed.

About four or five years later, I went to a lecture by the famous clairvoyant and healer Rosalyn L. Bruyere. She described her work with men who had experienced heart attacks early in life. She explained that in many, if not every, case, these men recalled having been visited by a woman spirit guide earlier in their lives but that they had ignored or suppressed the memory of the guide. The messages I received from this entire set of experiences were to trust my intuition, always pay attention to inner stirrings, and know that mystery is an integral and powerful part of life. I also believe that, at some deep level, the spirit of my mother was watching over me then and still is now as I write this more than forty years later.

All is Synchronicity

PART THREE
Deepening

Ode to Divinity

What if, without our own knowing,
we are each a vessel for some greater Being,
One who brought us here
to help others
we don't know and will never even meet?

The Christ, the anointed one,
asked for his cup to be taken.

The Buddha, perfectly self-awakened,
touched the earth and smiled.

The Sage, holder of the three treasures,
rose out of and sank back into the River.

Lord Krishna, the unmanifested,
gently smiled at the battlefield.

To be like them,
To know that not knowing is knowledge …

We were called
Here for this.

~J.B.

The preceding chapters defined the soul without reference to God. For many, presence to life may depend on faith, belief in, or experience of, God. For them, God animates soul, informs essence, lives before and after this fleeting incarnation, and lovingly calls us to acceptance, presence, self-transcendence, and selflessness. In other words, for many of us, there can be no soul or soulful capacity without God. Souls are the living sparks of God.

CHAPTER 7

An Intercession–
Calling the Divine Origin
of Soulful Capacities

call this chapter an intercession. It is my attempt to take a humble attitude when it comes to discussions about God and theology. I did not originally plan to write this chapter. It actually was the last chapter I wrote for this book. One day after reading through the entire manuscript, I came to the uncomfortable thought, "How can I write about the soul without at least mentioning God and divine forces behind the soul?" I then had this feeling. I was compelled to act on behalf of those faith-based and religious readers who would want to frame the Soulful Capacities in relationship to God.

This intercession is written for those with such faith, for those interested in how Presence might have divine qualities. And it is also written for atheists. Diversity of belief is a common mark of humanity. Regardless of whether you are a "believer" or "nonbeliever," I hope you discern an intuitive string that threads together another part of your own "happening life" map. At some level, we are all threaded together in the diversity of our beliefs.

Intercession

In common language, intercession means the act of intervening on the behalf of another and often for the benefit of the third party who is helped by the intercession.

101

In religion, particularly Christianity, an intercession or intercessory prayer, refers to praying for or inviting God's presence to come into the life of others (an individual, group, organization) to protect, guide, or bless those others.

Much of what we know of the Soulful Capacities comes from spiritual teachers who had a deeply intimate relationship to a god of their own understanding. This intimacy often blossomed outside religion or a system of faith or worship. These teachers sometimes founded a religion. They learned the Soulful Capacities through God, a higher power, or the deepest nature of reality.

The following sections draw parallels between the Soulful Capacities and diverse depictions of God. The parallels do not equate a Soulful Capacity with the dominion of any one religion. I am not specifically aligning Acceptance with Christ, Presence with Buddha, Flow with the Sages of Taoism, or Synchronicity with Krishna (Hinduism). These spiritual leaders taught all Soulful Capacities. One purpose of this intercession is to spark your curiosity about our common humanity or, actually, the unity of spirit woven into the multiplicity of faiths in every corner of this planet. The parallels are suggestions. Follow your own quest for presence, whether or not you ascribe to any faith.

Acceptance

Acceptance often arises after we lose or fail to achieve something of value. Pain and suffering emerge when our will cannot force things to go our way; they turn our attention away from our own limited perspective to something greater. In the evolution of humanity's consciousness, Acceptance transforms into the deepest surrender during great adversity and aloneness. This transformation is embodied in the life of Christ.

In the four Gospels of the Bible, the garden of Gethsemane is where Jesus prays to God before he is arrested on the evening before his crucifixion. Matthew 26:39 (NIV) reads, "Going a little farther, he fell with his face to the ground and prayed, 'My Father, if it is possible, may this cup be taken from me. Yet not as I will, but as you will.'" This experience, sometimes labeled the "Agony in the Garden," conveys how suffering is part of the human condition. "The cup," our very life, contains all that can or ever will happen to us. Jesus, in accepting his destiny, asks God to take his life to do with it according to God's will.

This prayer is echoed in more modern prayers. For example, in Alcoholics Anonymous, the Third-Step prayer reads, "God, I offer myself to Thee—to build with me and to do with me as Thou wilt. Relieve me of the bondage of self, that I may better do Thy will."

Presence

Presence occurs through the complete subsiding of ego. When attention is so deeply immersed in the moment, one tastes something sublime, ecstatic, divine. The immersion is all-encompassing; one's ego (fear, attachment, hate) is obliterated. Statues of Buddha show him sitting serenely, his left hand, palm facing upward, on his lap. His right hand is on his right knee with his fingers touching the earth. This touch is calling the earth to witness Buddha defying Mara, the god of birth, desire, and death.

Mara had tempted the Buddha while, according to traditional Buddhist texts the Buddha meditated without moving from his seat for forty-nine days under the bodhi tree. Mara tried everything to distract the Buddha from enlightenment. He sent his beautiful naked daughters to inspire lust, and an army of soldiers hurled thousands of spears and arrows to inspire fear. These weapons turned into flowers as they approached the compassionate presence of the Buddha. Mara also tried to inspire doubt by badgering, "Who do you think you are? You are nobody." The Buddha's enlightenment is tied up with the defeat of Mara, ending the cycle of suffering, birth, rebirth, and death.

Presence involves letting go of any attachment to the *idea* of a God or gods. Instead, we discover a direct and immediate relationship *to* God, the very ground of being. The Buddha never argued for or against God's existence, yet much Buddhist thought argues God would have to be eternal. Realizing there is no permanent self, we witness impermanence. Presence involves an ongoing, detached observation of all phenomena.

Flow

The human experience of Flow represents or mimics the state of Flow that exists within all of nature. Everything—the moments, the days, the seasons, the minerals, the animals, life, and death—is in a state of ever-constant change and Flow. Christians will sometimes report that they feel the Holy Spirit *flow* through them. Feeling that one is in a state of grace, of being without blame or sin, touches into the feeling that one is flowing with and blessed by God. There is no struggle because of regret or shame. We are redeemed. Flow is perhaps best captured in the philosophy of Taoism.

The Tao is defined as the hidden creative energy that animates the universe, the *ever-present* stream of existence. The Tao is the first principle of the universe, the all-embracing reality from which everything else arises. The Sage perceives the Tao, not through concepts, but only by stopping any striving. Through love, humility, and living in the moment-to-moment—the three treasures—one flows effortlessly and in a natural way with nature. Some aspects of Taoism indicate this practice can allow one to achieve immortality.

As with Buddhism, Taoism does not argue for or against the existence of God. The Sage knows the Tao cannot be named. Instead, we focus on being and recognize some ultimate spiritual force that cannot be directly known. However, we see the Tao in the manifest world of nature. The Tao is a unifying force, not unlike Western notions of God.

Synchronicity

The experience of Synchronicity, serendipity, or meaningful coincidence leaves us with a rich sense of destiny: "This meaningful event was predestined to happen just at this time. I could not have predicted it would happen, nor did I cause it." In the magic moment, we sense we are always being guided, and we forget our own will. We lose a sense of an agentic ego as causing any event that unfolds in our lives.

In the tradition of karma-yoga, some believe that after intense spiritual practice, we realize that predestination overrides every unfolding moment. From that point on, everything is a coming together of one meaningful moment after another. Karma-yoga, a path in Hinduism, encourages selfless action for the benefit of others. We dedicate work without attachment to the fruits of our labors and remain completely neutral to outcomes, whether success, failure, or anything else.

This attitude is taught by Lord Krishna in the Bhagavad Gita, the main source text of Hinduism. In it, Krishna claims, "The spirit soul bewildered by the influence of false ego thinks himself the doer of activities that are in actuality carried out by the three modes of material nature" (chapter 3: verse 27). "Material nature consists of the three modes—goodness, passion, and ignorance. When the living entity comes in contact with nature, ... he becomes conditioned by these modes" (chapter 14: verse 5). Krishna explains that we can practice goodness to attain higher realms, but we will only know God by transcending all three modes altogether and seeing that everything happens according to God's will.

Practicing the Presence of God

The above examples demonstrate how diverse teachers and traditions all distinguish between a false sense of self (ego) and a soul or the essential, spiritual force we embody as human beings; the examples we've discussed are the prayer in Gethsemane, the patient conquering of Mara, entering the ever-present Tao, and teaching the illusion of ego. Each point to a surrender of self. There can be no Presence without God's interceding between the soul and the ego.

Through the chapters that follow, readers might think that the Soulful Capacities can be cultivated completely on one's own through self-instruction, the application of will, and following the various exercises provided. Perhaps this is true to some extent. However, once we acknowledge a distinction between ego and soul or essence, we recognize something more profound at work. This power may be apprehended as the four Radiant Forces discussed in *QfP Book 1*. Here, let's call it God.

The Practice of the Presence of God is a compilation of conversations by Brother Lawrence (1605–1691), a Carmelite friar. This practice is a continuous prayer, a deep contemplation, of God's presence. The gist of Brother Lawrence's message was the importance of maintaining *repeated* efforts to keep *attention* on and *remember* God throughout the day, during all chores, in business, and in conversation. This practice did not begin or end with the work of Brother Lawrence and is seen in many traditions.

The practice of Presence in the Christian tradition appears to have its roots in *The Philokalia of the Holy Neptic Fathers*, a collection of texts written between the fourth and the fifteenth centuries by spiritual masters of the Orthodox Christian tradition. The word *nepsis* means an urgent command to stay ever wakeful, watchful, and vigilant. The vigilance refers to watching the mind whenever it is distracted by any thoughts, sensuality, worldly phenomena that take one's mind off the thought of God.

This practice of continuously returning to the thought of God is different from distinctive times set aside for "prayer" (for example, Muslim Salah; morning or evening prayer; Sabbath prayer). It is an ongoing attitude of recollection in order to absorb oneself in God. In this way, it is very much like: sadhana (a Hindi term for daily spiritual practice to communicate with God); Waheguru simran (repetition of God's names) in Sikhism; mantra in Hindu faiths; and, in the Jewish tradition, similar to tefillah (communion with God through a deep preparation, contemplation, and recognition of oneself in relation to God); and devekut (absorption into God). With so many similar practices, we may conclude that humanity has itself been on its own quest for quite some time.

The Divine Origin of Presence:
A Dialogue with Joseph Howell and Art Wimberly

Imagine that you were at your child's funeral. Even the most hard-hearted of us would find presence at a funeral of their mother or their child. At different moments in this life, we have at least small windows of loss, of awe, or of being close to death. This makes all of us present.

This quote came in a conversation with two of my colleagues from Alabama, Dr. Joseph Benton Howell and Arthur Wimberly (personal communication, October 23, 2020). Joe is the author of *Becoming Conscious: The Enneagram's Forgotten Passageway* and founder of the Institute of Conscious Being. Art is an addiction recovery coach and works with the Addiction Prevention Coalition in Birmingham, Alabama. I had asked both of them to speak with me because of something I had heard Joe say in a podcast.

The Enneagram has its origins as a tool for spiritual growth, for discerning between ego and essence. A modern focus of most Enneagram teaching has been on helping people identify their personality type, from a list of nine basic types or "ego fixations." In the podcast, Joe shared his experience of a recent Enneagram conference, where teachers avoided discussion about God and the soul. There was a drift away from spiritual discernment. At the least, teachers wanted to facilitate insight and enjoyable discussions about personality. At most, the Enneagram could be used to help students deal with the challenge of their own particular ego-type. But God was off the table.

My conversation with Joe and Art came because I was writing this section on the divine origin of Presence. I was personally struggling with my own discernment; how to introduce God into an objective map for navigating time in this brief life. We talked about whether it is important to reach those whose quest had no place for God. I was concerned that this section on God might lose readers. At one point, Art recalled passages from chapter 10:14 in the Gospel of Matthew

(NIV): "*If anyone will not welcome you or listen to your words, leave that home or town and shake the dust off your feet.*"

As we continued to talk, we discussed other, more modern approaches to the divine origins of Presence. Joe referenced the Russian philosopher George Ivanovich Gurdjieff, considered one of the original teachers of the Enneagram. Joe shared:

Real presence undergirds the mind, heart, and body. One can come to presence through any of these spiritual centers. The soul activates these centers so that they act simultaneously, align, and coordinate in order to allow the divine to enter into our life. This is known as Gurdjieff's Fourth Way. The soul activates the wholeness of the human being and brings these different centers together at the same time. This can happen through any method, at any time: through Tai Chi, yoga, meditation, or simply sitting and being with another person.

Gurdjieff's Fourth Way refers to the integration of three spiritual methodologies to awaken one's consciousness (that is, to be present). These are the methods of the *fakir*, from Sufism, and refer to someone who continually repeats the names of God (dhikr) with complete surrender of one's heart to God; the *monk* who is ever watchful of emotions and keeps God above all else; and the *yogi* who seeks to conquer the mind or relinquish its hold on our life through diverse mental and physical practices.

We also discussed the concept of "The Holy Instant" in *A Course in Miracles* (*ACIM*). This is a three-volume curriculum developed through the Foundation for Inner Peace and consists of a text, a workbook for students, and a manual for teachers. *ACIM* teaches a way to universal love and peace—or remembering God. Joe reflected on the use of the word "appearances" in *ACIM*.

What appears to be bad or good is only how it appears. In truth, the reality of what happens in our life is only for the purpose of healing and wholeness. Appearance is a judgment by the ego. If we stay in ego, we categorize appearances into good, bad, indifferent. The miracle of the Holy Instant is that there really are no categories, no room for judging and reacting. The ego functions to set up categories. Instead, we should enjoy the miracle of each instant. As soon as one categorizes or judges experience, presence goes away. It is called the "Holy" Instant because we are bringing in the divine. This means we cannot truly talk about presence without bringing in God and the divine.

We then talked about why so many are not present to life, whether or not God is involved. Our conversation touched on the artificial representations of Presence in the world of commercialism, buying, selling, and massive attempts to capture our attention and "presence" as consumers. There are many false gods and false gurus. Social media, virtual presentations, the constant barrage of advertisements are just a few, and all have the intention of capturing people's attention to be "present" to *my* product, *my* message, or *my* channel. Even the growing use of artificial intelligence is part; our "presence" is being co-opted by the world.

Joe suggested, *"The more we define presence as a divine, soulful, holy thing, the more it contrasts with what people think is presence."* We talked about how, beginning in the 1950s, the modern science of psychology and psychiatry steered away from discussions of God. Psychology became a modern science that divorced itself from spiritual matters. The focus turned toward behavior, measurement, and how to treat people with drugs. At that point, some turned to the use of hallucinogens (LSD) to "bypass God" and as a move away from the social norms of modern psychological research. Joe recalled how in the 1960s and 1970s, it was completely taboo to speak of the divine and psychological healing in the secular world.

Joe then referred to M. Scott Peck's book *The Road Less Traveled* (originally published in1978) and how it brought about a renewed conversation between science and religion. Subtitled *A New Psychology of Love, Traditional Values, and Spiritual Growth*, Peck's book was on the *New York Times* Bestseller list for more than eleven years (598 consecutive weeks) and is estimated to have sold more than ten million copies worldwide.

The book balances science and religion. Peck referred to the latter as a "worldview" that significantly influences our attitudes toward life, love, and discipline. Neither science nor religion are superior, and grace is a mysterious force of positive growth in our lives.

Joe shared:

This book was very popular. It showed that if we want to change, we must not only rely on our common sense but also on a power greater than ourselves. Peck allowed it to be socially acceptable for more people to talk about God than was previously true for many people in that generation. There are other modern popular authors who have echoed Peck's advice. Each of these authors suggest that, in the final analysis, true seekers will always give credence to the fact that we are not alone, that we don't understand ourselves.

As Art, Joe, and I finished our conversation, we came back to the idea of audience: Who am I trying to reach with this book about the quest for presence? Regarding my concern that I might lose readers if we place too much emphasis on the soul, Joe remarked:

If we talk about presence in the divine, the people you will lose are those who think that humans have it all together, have it all sewn up, and are their own healing agents. It is my experience that the vast majority of people have some inkling that there is more to the appearances of this happening life. We are all part of the human enterprise. The "other" can always be reached. There is something about presence that awakens the spirit in anyone.

CHAPTER 8

Contemplations

Ode to the Bending Grass

The Sage wrote:
Whichever way the wind blows, the grass bends.
As one discerns its ever-changing trace,
why should one worry about the unseen wind?
There is so much beauty
even now
when it stops to whisper to you

~J.B.

Contemplations are a lost art. We often suffer for the lack of Contemplation. We rush, fail to take our time, miss out on life's Treasures, and forget how precious life is. We can recover this lost art through signposts and practices. We can learn this together, and we can find the Treasures with each other.

The history of our human race appears to have been moving in a line from the past to the future. This image of history and our evolution as a species—as only following time's arrow—is only a metaphor, a tool, a mistake. The truth is more complex, more thrilling. You can align your life with this truth. Your life—your story—also may appear to be a straight line. Yet, some part of you knows that there is a whole lot more going on than can be captured in any single, straight line. There are many layers. To see these clearly, it helps to take different perspectives.

Think about any music you have enjoyed, such as from a band, a jazz ensemble, or a symphony. Now consider this music from two perspectives. From a logical, linear, rational, or analytic perspective, music comes from distinct notes on a page, a series of digits, marks, and notations. As each note is played, it has a timbre, rises and falls in volume, lingers and blends with the previous and the next note. From a sensory and immersive perspective, those notes blend and weave together and create a full and complete experience that arouses feelings, emotions, memories, and even actions.

Now, consider moments in time: seconds on a clock or a digital display. Our experience of life is not just a succession and accumulation of these fractions of clock-time. We wade through, dance with, and experience many layers from moment to moment in our life. However, we tend to be less aware of these moment-to-moment *wadings*. We have a better sense of how we move from one situation or occasion to another: from home to work, from work to the grocery store, from home to the gym, from using our devices (computer, smartphone, television) to paying more attention to each other.

This happening life is made up of these interlacing movements. This is the life that we are called to be present to. Unfortunately, many of us succumb to clock-time. We only see or believe that time is chronological in nature. In truth, our life is more like the experience of the song—rhapsody or symphony—than of reading notes on a page. Even if you are fully alive with that fact—and it is a fact—you will still benefit from Contemplation. You may discover Flow and even timelessness, transcend time altogether, and embrace other Treasures within this very life you are living.

But perhaps you feel like you are caught on a treadmill, anchored to your smartphone, or stuck in a time prison. You may want more meaning and fullness in your life, more perspective, and more control of your time. If so, you are encouraged and challenged to contemplate— that is, reflect, let your mind meander, take time to consider, chew on, and otherwise embrace different perspectives and approaches. The ideas presented here come from many perspectives, such as philosophy, teachers, and science. Among these—and for the sake of explaining more about Contemplation—it will help to know a little about the Chinese *Book of Changes*, otherwise known as the *I Ching*.

The *I Ching* is a Chinese classic text describing an ancient system of cosmology and philosophy. The *I Ching* is at the heart of traditional Chinese cultural beliefs. One dictionary defines it as "an ancient Chinese manual of divination based on eight symbolic trigrams and sixty-four hexagrams, interpreted in terms of the principles of yin and yang." Feel free to explore any book or website on the *I Ching*. There are dozens of interpretations available.

REFLECTION

I was introduced to the *I Ching* by two friends in my life, both by the name of Ken: Kenny Macklin (a childhood friend who I still talk with) and Kenneth Phillips (a polymath, pianist, philanthropic lover of koalas, and somewhat of an expert on the *I Ching*). Ken Phillips was executive vice president of telecommunications for Citicorp, which he rarely talked about. He wrote a chapter, "The Riddle of Change," about the parallels between the sixty-four *I Ching* hexagrams and the sixty-four codons of our genetic code (in *Studies in Nondeterministic Psychology*, edited by Gerald Epstein, 1980; ACMI Press).

I met Ken P. in my sophomore year in college (1976) while taking the train from White Plains to New York City. We became friends and spent many hours in conversation. I am grateful that Ken introduced me to the Italian café (Café Degli Artisti in New York's Greenwich Village) long before there was such a thing as Starbucks. Even now, I rarely have a latte or cannoli without having some strand of memory pulled by Ken.

The *I Ching* is mentioned here to explain more about Contemplation and its importance as a lost art. This art is becoming more precious in a world overloaded with constant digital, sensory, and electronic messages that keep us stuck in linear time. Time in the *Í Ching* is amazing in several ways. For example, it shows how life can transition in ways that reflect nature, the seasons, and the elements. Our current circumstances (whether joyful or miserable) may hold the seed of the opposite condition, the timing of which emerges in systematic ways. And by attuning to the Rhythm and Flow of life's natural changes, we can cultivate wisdom and strengthen our character.

One of the hexagrams (Hexagram 20) is titled "Contemplation," and it looks like the image on the right. It is made up of two trigrams, groups of three letters that represent a sound. (The Above Trigram is *Sun* the Gentle, Wind; The Below Tri-  gram is *K'un* the Receptive, Earth). The image is of wind blowing across the earth, and interpretations of this image often reference surveying the pattern of the bending and weaving of the grass. It is to remind us that to see things as they truly are, we must be still and observe the unfolding of moments from a place of inner stillness. Moment to moment, time slips away.

One of the most well-known writings in the *Í Ching* (translated by Richard Wilhelm) reads: *"When the wind blows over the earth it goes far and wide, and the grass must bend to its power."* A person who is attuned to this will be able to read the real sentiments of others and discern truth from deception. Further, because of this ability, their personality will be impactful and sway others, just as the grass is swayed by the wind.

Wilhelm's translation distinguishes six ways that Contemplation can manifest, corresponding to the six lines of the hexagram. Here are the translations of the six lines, along with my interpretations of each:

1. **See the Big Picture (Totality).** Contemplate life from a distance to understand how specific events are a connected part of a greater whole. Even if others do not understand your "big picture" perspective, do your best to avoid being shallow and taking too much time with shallow things. This means that you don't look at life

like an innocent or immature child. Rather, you understand the seriousness of the opportunity you have been given to be alive and take a long-term view instead of getting caught up in the moment. You seek to understand how deeper forces may be at work in your life. *QfP Book 1* describes four of these deeper forces and how they inform our daily lives and our personalities.

2. **It Is Not About You.** Always be mindful that your vantage point is limited, especially when dealing with others in the public sphere. We all tend to see how things relate to ourselves—a self-serving bias. In doing so, you limit your ability to take the perspective of others. Instead, you can empathize or show compassion when it may be essential to do so. Many exercises contained herein (Contemplations) encourage you to take perspectives other than your own.

3. **Observe.** Make an effort toward self-contemplation, self-awareness, and objectivity. This does not mean preoccupation with your own thoughts but being mindful of the effects that your thoughts create (on your emotions, perspectives, and actions). Through self-observation, you can act with more wisdom in your dealings. This is also called "skillful means." You can better determine when to move ahead with something, when to pause, or when to take a step back. Time Shaping (*QfP Book 1*) is one of the four deeper forces that make up the weave of this happening life. Through observation, you can pace, schedule, and craft routines that bring wisdom.

4. **Bring Out the Best in Others.** Contemplate the positive potential of the situation you and others are in. Reflect on what actions will lead you and your community to thrive and flourish. The best attitude is one of being a guest and exercising a sense of honor and respect. Approaching others with a sense of honor and respect for their inherent expertise encourages sharing of their gifts and talents.

5. **Be the Change You Want to See.** As part of self-contemplation, be mindful that your personality may have defects or areas that you can improve upon as you move forward in life. This attitude helps

cultivate a non-defensive and disarming way of interacting with others. This does not mean you should give in to negative self-talk. Rather, by contemplating all aspects of yourself, you can devote your time to essential matters instead of wasting time on the past. As a result, you create your own reality.

6. **Find Life's Treasures Beyond Yourself.** Contemplate those aspects of life that are without ego, selfishness, or self-centeredness. Look for and share the Treasures of life that all people can experience: Preciousness, Awe, Spontaneity, Beauty, Love. They are everywhere. The more that you practice the previous five Contemplations, the more likely these Treasures will naturally emerge.

Contemplation (QfP 2-6): Practicing Contemplation

Here are suggested exercises for you to practice Contemplation:

1. **Journal:** Reflect on the six concepts described above. If you had to select one as most important or most needed in your life right now, which one would you select? What would be next on the list? Continue in this way until you have rank ordered all six. Then journal about your top-ranked area for each, then revisit the list, and journal on each in order.

2. **Nature:** Go outside or watch nature from your window, paying continuous attention to the natural, inherent, and ongoing changes you see there: wind blowing over the grass or over a patch of water (river, lake, ocean); the trees, a flower, or bush as it shifts with the wind; the passing of clouds; the shadows of the day; birds, squirrels, insects as they scurry and flip around. Take some time to do this.

3. **Life:** Reflect on where you are today—this day—in the magnificent stream of your entire life. What is special about this day? Where does it fit in terms of the day before and the day to follow?

CHAPTER 9

Temple

Ode to Dear Kairos

The Spartan runner, The Town Crier
From the Center of the Square,
You hear this at the right time:

"All ye who hear this, may you honor that
    within you which is hearing this and
    then, dear ones, quickly note that this
    has already come and gone."

Yes, to honor, not like the idol sacrament.

But like the shaft of light pouring now
    from your eyes.
The waft of air exiting now from your ears
and touring about.

Light and air.
These temples we live in.

~J.B.

Figuratively speaking, a temple is a place set aside from the temporal (time-bound) world for one to contemplate the eternal. To see our time here as a holy place, a temple, increases our chances of uncovering (stumbling upon) life's Treasures. The idea of "place" inheres in our understanding of a temple as a space. The words temporal, contemplation, and temple all have the same etymological root and refer to *temp* from Proto-Italic *tempos*, meaning "to stretch, measure"; *tem*, "to cut," as in the notion of "place reserved or cut out"; and *contemplation*, from the Latin *contemplatio*, originally meaning "to mark out a space for observation."

We come into this world, it seems, as a separate (cut-off) body. But wherever you (and your body) go, there you are. So, this life is also a temple of time. We see this much more clearly when we get past our pursuit of things—even our own health, our need to be whole. The temple is revealed when we set aside time, cut off from the rest, to contemplate our impermanence against the widening sky. You are always in it, whether you know it or not.

Many people believe the ultimate goal of life's journey lies in the meaningful fulfillment of some cherished value, accomplishment, realization, or legacy—whether in family, service, career, or one's own private aspiration. Others think that such activities and aspirations are fleeting and what matters most is access to higher states of being, insight into the flourishing and eternal cosmos, touching or merging with the divine, surrendering oneself. These two world views are not mutually exclusive; they do not depend on religious belief, and they actually nourish each other.

Self-Transcendence

The psychologist Abraham Maslow viewed two distinct ways of being: *self-actualization* (fulfillment of personal potential) and *self-transcendence* (expanding beyond the boundaries of oneself). These influence and even define our health. Indeed, the word *health* has the same origin as the words for whole and holy. Can we be healthy without some integration of our whole and spiritual nature? But beyond that, we may learn that all of humanity, especially the complex design of our DNA, brains, and nervous systems, is a simple manifestation of cosmic consciousness residing throughout the universe.

The past twenty years have seen growth in the scientific study of self-transcendence and its relationship to well-being. In the field of psychology, self-transcendence is a central topic in three peer-reviewed journals: *The Journal of Humanistic Psychology* (founded in 1961), *The Journal of Transpersonal Psychology* (founded in 1969), and *The Journal of Positive Psychology* (founded in 2006). Self-transcendence studies are growing in other fields: holistic nursing, hospice studies, aging (gerontology), and psycho-oncology.

The study of human growth and consciousness contains many broad and open-ended constructs, such as resilience, intimacy, and love. Most current science—stuck in a reductionist and operational paradigm—will struggle to agree on a common definition of these ideas. The same is true for spiritual health. When it comes to any aspect of spirituality, it may be nearsighted and self-limiting to use only one definition. What might be even worse is to act as though we know what we are talking about when it comes to transcendent matters.

Your Personal Quest

Instead, and for this brief orientation, do your own personal quest. Let's look at some of the self-report questionnaires—what scientists study when they measure self-transcendence and spiritual health. Below is a random selection of items typically endorsed by people who are considered to be *moving in the direction of* or *evolving toward* spiritual health or self-transcendence. Review these items with the intent of self-assessment. Do you agree with them?

1. I am able to reach deep down into myself for comfort.

2. A higher spiritual power or being is a source of help and direction in my life.

3. I spend a portion of every day in prayer, meditation, and/or personal reflection.

4. It seems that my life has always had purpose.

5. I have had moments of great joy in which I suddenly had a clear, deep feeling of oneness with all that exists.

6. Often, when I look at an ordinary thing, something wonderful happens—I get the feeling that I am seeing it fresh for the first time.

7. I feel that my individual life is a part of a greater whole.

8. I am able to move beyond things that once seemed important.

9. I believe that death is a doorway to another plane of existence.

10. No matter where I am or what I'm doing, I am never separate from others.

11. At the most basic level of reality, everything is one.

These items come from existing research surveys. Notice a difference between items 1 to 4 and items 5 to 11. The first set comes from measures of *spiritual health* or *spiritual well-being*, whereas the latter set comes from questionnaires that measure *self-transcendence* or one's ability to have experiences that go beyond the self. Item 9, seeing "death as a doorway," speaks directly to the awareness of the soul. The soul knows that the body is impermanent and that our ego and personality are limited.

Both types of questionnaires are used in studies on how to better treat patients, in hospice work, and in research on death and dying. Spiritual health and self-transcendence complement and nourish each other, especially as we get older. I believe it is essential that we always use both approaches (personally and in our careers).

When Is the Temple?

The word *kadosh* (holy) is used for the first time in the Book of Genesis at the end of the story of creation. How extremely significant is the fact that it is applied to time: "And God blessed the seventh day and made it holy." There is no reference in the record of creation to any object in space that would be endowed with the quality of holiness.

~ABRAHAM JOSHUA HESCHEL (POLISH-BORN AMERICAN RABBI)

There was a time (in history, in most religions) when we were called, even told, to take some time to completely stop the quest, cease pursuing, or even just rest with an abiding gratitude for life and the universe. For most of society, this time is "cut off from the rest of the week" and called a "day of rest" or "Sabbath." Over time, and through modern commercial society, the day of rest evolved into the "weekend" as a time to rest from work, a time for leisure but not necessarily to contemplate life. And the "siesta" emerged as a way to take a rest or a nap in the middle of the day, originating as a break from heat or hard work or due to the drowsiness brought on by the midday meal.

Many religious traditions carve out routines where followers pray, worship, or honor spiritual or divine principles and entities. The Jewish Sabbath is one example of a weekly "set-aside." There are many other forms, including going to church on Sunday in the Christian tradition, daily prayers in Islam, and annual holidays and days of remembering. In most cases, these times and days are related to attendance in a place-temple, mosque, church, or other house of worship.

So, on the one hand—from the world of work and industry—we have time to take a break. On the other hand—from the world of religion and spirituality—we have time for worship. In both cases, time is treated as a segment: a part that is distinct from the rest of our day, our week, our year. Equating this time with a place (such as a church) helps many people feel a bodily sense that their attendance represents or symbolizes a true honoring of the divine. Effort and responsibility are required to attend—to be *present* in—God's place.

But *what if you do not have a place? What if you are homeless, either literally or spiritually?* Reflect on these questions from the viewpoints of both self-actualization and self-transcendence.

Imagine you seek self-actualization—to be the best and most complete and healthy self you were born to be. If there were no houses of worship (or perhaps you did not believe in them), you might go about creating a time and place for spiritual health—such as worship, yoga, meditation, prayer, contemplative practice, or time connecting with nature. These are things you can certainly do. Studies show they can help greatly with not only your own health and well-being but also the health and well-being of those with whom you might interact and for whom you might be a role model.

Alternately, imagine your interest lies solely in self-transcendence —to experience oneness, wholeness, timelessness, joy—regardless of any benefit these experiences might bring. Instead of doing any practice, you might first ask,

+ *What if I don't even need a place?*

+ *What if "God's place" is everywhere?*

+ *What if "God's place" is every time?*

The Dungeon in the Temple

Self-transcendence is not the only path on which our soul awakens from time. There is also a path down into the depths and darkness. Grief, anguish, despair, depression—encountering loss, failure, trauma—also catalyze. And there is the shadow. We can deny, ignore, or hide from aspects of ourselves we find unacceptable: addictions, family secrets, hate toward others (projections of our own dark side), and vices such as greed, chauvinism, jealousy, or long-held resentments. Some of us find the truth not at the temple's altar but in the hidden corners of the basement.

Contemplation (Q*f*P 2-7): Temple

1. Reflect on the three questions about place just above. What is your answer?

2. When have you last honored the Sabbath (or any day set-aside)? Can you do so now?

3. Review the eleven statements on self-transcendence and spiritual health. How do you answer these differently? Can you tell the difference between them in your life?

CHAPTER 10

The Veil

Ode to Reveal

Does the clock just tick? Or does it tickle?
Metronome? Alarm? Wake-up call?
Gloss over? Go back to sleep?
Or Voyage on Through?

Time: the final frontier.

These are the voyages of
the Starship (Put Your Name Here).

Your continuing mission:
to explore new time,
to seek out new perspectives on time, and
to boldly show up where
no one has shown up before.

To remove the Veil.

~J.B.

For many centuries, we have used space, not time, to understand the world around us. As a result, time is not what we think it is. Not even close. The concepts of time that humanity has concocted to get us all to this point of civilization and evolution—however far along you think we may be—are only a thin slice of reality. Time covers; it is a Veil. We live and work on the surface while other forces play behind the Veil. These include physical, chemical, geological, cosmological, and "man-made" forces.

We have grown accustomed to the overlay of **routines, schedules,** and calendars; these nested units of time afford a sense of control and order: seconds, minutes, hours, days, weeks, months, years, decades, centuries, millennia, epochs, and so on. This metaphor—of these units nested within each other—captures a sense that these are knitted together, like a veil, a weave.

The Veil of time, however, also includes our sense or use of rhythm, timing, and **pacing**, our understanding that things and processes have **transitions** or phases, and our perceptions and awareness that these aspects can come together—synchronize or entrain with each other. We may know whether our **rhythm** is on or off, whether the **timing** is right, whether we are moving too fast or too slow, are patient or impatient. We may know when it is time to come or go, to arrive or depart, to make a change or to stay. We may know when things are working well with others or on a project or whether they are out of kilter.

The Veil includes aspects that allow us to get a glimpse of broader and deeper aspects of time. This includes times when we are interrupted, when there is some disturbance, when something happens out of the ordinary. We often experience this as newness or novelty—usually through some intentional leisure pursuit or entertainment of some kind. But many **interruptions** occur without notice or control, such as death, accidents, disasters, and pandemics. The suddenness or unexpected nature of these experiences communicates a wider reality about the temporary nature of our existence. Grief and humility open us up beyond our ordinary rhythms.

The Veil of time also includes moments of **transcendence**, often fleeting or precious. We savor life, take time to smell the roses, and feel Awe, Contentment, Fulfillment, Spontaneity, or a sublime Flowing *with* life. Thus, the Veil of time is itself a rich tapestry of experiences through which the soul sometimes peeks. Because of death, the Veil is a precious one, like a very fine fabric, a gossamer. We mostly experience life through it rather than directly; and we mostly act like it is not there rather than discern its patterns.

The soul is covered by a thousand veils.

~Hazrat Inayat Khan (Indian poet and Sufi teacher)

Is it time to see the Veil and then pierce it? *Are you ready to continue on your mission, to boldly go where no one has gone before? Are you not alone in that mission?*

Contemplation (QfP 2-8): The Veil

1. Have you ever sensed that "the happenings" of this world are just on the surface? If so, what prompted the experience? If not, what is your opinion about the possibility that it is all a Veil?

2. Note the eight words **bolded** on the previous page. Take a moment to recall a recent experience of each and reflect on and sense its influence on you. What does *routine* feel like? How did you sense a recent *transition* in your life? Take a step back and view any of these experiences from a distance. (Book 4 reviews these in depth.)

3. Many stories and films convey a distinction between the "appearances" of this world and the unseen forces that drive everything. Some dystopian science fiction includes *The Matrix* trilogy (1999-2003) and *Person of Interest* (TV Series, 2011-2016). Other, more spiritual stories suggest an underlying destiny or magic to the events of the world. Two examples are the British television series *Merlin* (2008) and *Cloud Atlas* (2004 book by David Mitchell, and 2012 movie).

Exercise: Watch or read diverse versions of the "surface-hidden" distinction with other people. Ask them to read this chapter and reflect on the following questions:

1. How is time itself (for example, clock-time, our routines) also a Veil?

2. How can we pierce it?

CHAPTER 11

Preciousness

Ode to This Holding That

I am never done with fragility.
Fragility will definitely be done with me

All these gurus say "be vulnerable."
Others say "suck it up."
I don't get it.
I have never held anything different.
It is all the same.

Water slipping through my fingers.

~J.B.

REFLECTION

I have been married for close to twenty-five years. Throughout this time, and with some regularity, I demonstrate both impatience when my wife takes her time with everyday things as well as anger when our time together is interrupted. Going to the grocery store with her is a major challenge for me. For all my teaching on the topic of Presence, I react, and it is not pretty. Across all the many domestic situations I share as a marriage partner, I have been less patient and serene than otherwise. The practice of *just being with* is difficult. And yet there is a place, a container, between my holding it together and my getting caught up in anger and impatience. Somehow the institution of marriage saves me; the commitment to "keep showing up no matter what" makes a difference. I experience a stark, cold fragility when I judge her, argue, withdraw, make her into the villain. Thankfully, I come back to a sense of humility. The very fragility I fear gives birth to a sense of how precious our time is. I often wonder if others have people in their own family who test their patience and make it a challenge to just be present.

There comes a point in the fragility of a thing when we start to notice and have an opportunity to respond with care, with listening, with mindfulness. So many things go the way of fragility and open us to the potential of Preciousness. Consider the paint chips in an old building, the crisped leaves of a neglected plant, and the restive baby left in the sun too long who squirms and whines. These are more ordinary than the melting of the glaciers and other problems brought on by climate change. Our contact and intimacy with the way things age, with their vulnerability and their exposure, makes them more than things. Attentiveness and compassion initiate an ongoing renewal, a nurturing and a protection, that may otherwise never unfold. Intimacy is born in even just the hint of this cherishing, where the aging of things meets a cradle of care, where we sense that we are all subject to time's flow.

Rushing around from one activity to another, we generally do not take the time for this kind of intimacy. The common complaint is that one never has enough time to do all that one wants or needs. We keep ourselves too busy to think about or spend time with the precious things of life. But it isn't that we don't have enough time; rather, it is because we think of time solely as something we can possess (for example, measure, spend, or buy time) that we have created a world of pressure, deadlines, and appointments. The issue lies not with time itself but in how we think about it and speak about it, using careless metaphors in our conversations and everyday language.

Instead of thinking of time as a quantity that is objective and separate or as an end to be reached, we can think of it more poetically as an abiding quality. Again, I offer that we think of time in new ways. For example, we can think of time as the source of Preciousness in all things. Seen in this way, no longer is only our time precious, but time itself becomes precious.

With an awareness of such impermanence, our sense of separateness may dissolve: We really see just how fragile it all is. We learn that time and intimacy are interconnected. The inevitable decay of this world holds suffering in all that we are able to touch and for all that touches us. Here is our interconnectedness. For if we are all separate egos left only to ourselves, our portals of self-resilience, self-protection, we will fail to grow together. Time's flow will be seen only as decay and never yield the insight of Preciousness.

This way of understanding time may be clear to those of you who have looked deeply into your lover's eyes or held your newborn child. Many of us also know it through simple communication, through sharing the routines of daily life or participating in the gradual creation of our collective stories. Human contact, in all its many forms, hints at something essential, something alive and precarious. When love comes with its honor of the delicate, we create or embrace a context for each other's pain—the pain of decay, of loss, and of death. In each moment of our mutual gaze, we can transform fragility into Preciousness.

Time can become our companion or guide rather than a method for structuring our lives (through a schedule or calendar). It is much easier to understand the concept of eternity when we view time as something precious rather than as something we measure. Those who fall in love, mystics, and those in a state of rapture have felt this sense of eternity. What once caused these individuals to notice—the once fragile and later precious beloved—begins to radiate throughout all of time and so becomes timeless. From this height of intimacy, human beings throughout history have reported seeing and understanding both change and permanence. Many religious writers and philosophers recognize both impermanence—that all things do pass—and permanence—there is something connecting and passing within all things. This Passing has been given many names—the Tao, God, the Unconditioned, the Absolute, Eternity, the Indivisible. In spiritual writing, this Passing recedes or moves into an indescribable Receptacle—the Void, Emptiness, the Unobstructed, the Great Goddess, the Mother of All Things.

Of course, eternity is perhaps understood only by mystics and believed in only by the truly devout, the truly spiritual. I have wanted to show that it is possible to think about time other than in the ordinary ways to which we have confined ourselves. I also wanted to introduce the idea that time and intimacy are related in different ways: when we encounter something fragile and respond with care, when—through the desire for ongoing care—we feel that something is precious, when we appreciate the impermanence of all things of which we are a part, and when—through a shift in consciousness or spiritual encounter—we sense or come to believe in something that endures forever. Intimacy, in each of these experiences, meets for the purpose of meeting. It lives purely in the meeting, in the purity of knowing what it meets and as it meets. Intimacy itself is not about capturing, fixing, or transcending; for then, the Preciousness goes.

Contemplation (QfP 2-9): Preciousness

Exercise: Find an object in your home or office that is precious. Think about a person you know whom you consider precious. Select a work of art or culture that you consider precious. Recall an experience in your life that was particularly precious. What do you notice about each of these? What differences are there?

CHAPTER 12

Soulful Capacities Together and Personality

Ode to the Whole Time

You have been here the whole time
and didn't even know it,

Or has the whole of time taken you in
and wrapped itself around you?

Or, perhaps, nothing is really ever
    complete
on this strange soul-finding mission?

Stop asking for a moment;

you might just get caught off guard
by your own wholeness
while searching for something else.

~J.B.

In the *Quest for Presence*, personality is defined by *how* we express our Presence (and the other Soulful Capacities) in *unique* ways and as a *reflection* of deeper universal forces. This last chapter helps you summarize your insights and scores from the four chapters on Soulful

Capacities (chapters 3, 4, 5, and 6). The current chapter is devoted to one single Contemplation and provides a transition to *QfP Book 3* about personality. That Contemplation requires that you tally and integrate all your scores from the four previous self-assessments.

This total assessment of the Soulful Capacities is the first part of the *Quest for Presence Inventory*™ (QFPI™), which is designed to spark insight into your personality; specifically, how you express your Presence in unique ways. Book 3 provides the second part of the QFPI™, where you will explore nine different ways through which individuals are attracted to time as a positive resource for growth and fulfillment.

Your personality contains many unique features; however, it is limited as it is only a reflection of your essence. The soul or essence is unlimited and whole in and of itself. One reason we explore Soulful Capacities first (here in Book 2) is to give the soul the greater emphasis it deserves in a world of conversations that otherwise focus too much on personality. Most approaches to personality fail to explain human traits in the context of essence. The question, "What is the purpose of my personality?" is central to the *Quest for Presence*.

Contemplation (QfP 2-10): Soulful Capacities Together

If you have not already done so, go back to each of the four self-assessment exercises and complete them. Your total score for each will range from 20 to 100 points. Once you have completed them all, plot your scores on the following graph.

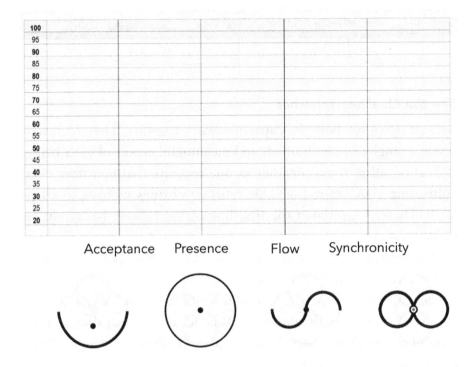

	Acceptance	Presence	Flow	Synchronicity
100				
95				
90				
85				
80				
75				
70				
65				
60				
55				
50				
45				
40				
35				
30				
25				
20				

Review the scores and their relative "height" to each other. Pay attention to what you notice about *both* the scores and your reactions to seeing any differences that exist.

You can ask yourself these questions as you ponder the pattern your plotted points reveal.

+ What is the first thing that I notice about my scores?

+ What appears high or low?

+ What is the first thing I notice in myself?

+ How does the overall feedback make me feel?

Next, review any of the four chapters and write your favorite quote, specific items from the self-assessment, or any phrase that captures your thoughts and feelings in the spaces below. For example, notice if you scored lower in one of the four areas. Which quote or phrase can you use as a reminder to strengthen that capacity?

Acceptance	Presence	Flow	Synchronicity

See the Qualities Together

Let's pause to see how the capacities work together. They each represent a single, whole, unified, and meaningful aspect of your being. Reflect on all of these together as one capacity that you have been cultivating your entire life. This reflection brings us back to chapter 8. There, I translated the first line of the *I Ching* hexagram on *Contemplation*:

Contemplate life from a distance to understand how specific events are a connected part of a greater whole.

No capacity is better or less than another. If you see that a score is lower in one area than another, this does not mean that you are lacking or less than others. Instead, focus on all positive aspects that are present.

Our soul or essence is one or unified. Whether we perceive it or not, we are always one with our soul or essence. We began, through previous chapters, by reviewing each capacity as separate to help us discern each as a means to get back in touch with our wholeness. As explained earlier, there is a deep relationship between our consciousness, our soul, and our capacity for experiencing soul in the world around us. By definition, our essence is always there, always with us. In chapter 2, we defined soul:

The soul is that inherent and unified aspect of a living being that contains or enfolds information from the entire universe.

So, now it is time to reflect on your overall and unified capacity for Acceptance, Presence, Flow, and Synchronicity. Together, these help to bring forward a sense of connection that, at some level, you already knew was there from the beginning. Consider these statements, each one taken from the self-assessments found in the contemplations of earlier chapters.

I feel a sense of fulfillment from just allowing life to happen.

I feel a deep connection to the wonders of nature.

I am good at savoring the simple and good things.

I see the deeper meaning of events.

What do all of these have in common? They point to an inner knowing that always has been within us. We tend to forget this knowing, often because we identify with our outer-self, our mask, our persona, our personality. When we experience true Acceptance (fulfillment), Presence (connection), Flow (savoring), and Synchronicity (meaning), we are in touch with the wholeness that is already there. All mystics guide us to this place.

> *O friend, you are infused with the Beloved –*
> *Just as fragrance is in a flower*
> *and the soul resides within the body,*
> *as fire is inherent in wood and redness in henna leaves,*
> *as clay is in a pot and butter in milk.*
> ~SANT CHARANDAS (18TH CENTURY INDIAN AND HINDU
> RELIGIOUS TEACHER) (SHRI BHAKTI SAGAR) (SHANGARI, 2014)

> *The soul always knows what to do to heal itself.*
> *The challenge is to silence the mind.*
> ~CAROLINE MYSS (AMERICAN AUTHOR)

You don't have to act crazy anymore
We all know you were good at that.

Now retire, my dear,
From all that hard work you do

Of bringing pain to your sweet eyes and heart.

Look in a clear mountain mirror
See the Beautiful Ancient Warrior
And the Divine elements
You always carry inside

That infused this universe with sacred Life
So long ago ...

~HAFIZ (14TH CENTURY PERSIAN AND SUFI POET)

So, contemplate this possibility: You are infused with the beloved, your soul knows what to do, and you always carry divine elements inside of you.

Your Score as a Whole

As part of this contemplation, review all the scores again from your self-assessments and total them all together. You will have one number that ranges from 80 to 400. Again, it does not matter what your score is. All you are doing right now is getting a sense. There are no criteria. There is no comparison point. This is not a scientific exercise where we are comparing numbers. It is only a very rough estimate anyway. You are your own assessor. The only person that needs to know your score is you. There is no judgment or criticism.

Take the opportunity to reflect on the total score as though you were reflecting an underlying and unified capacity to live through your essence or soul. You are finding that inherent fragrance, looking into that clear mountain lake mirror. Remember, the purpose of this happening life is to empower you to engage with a deeper and more whole sense of time. You are on a journey. These exercises (and your score) are a map. Once the terrain is revealed, place the map in your back pocket.

Your Score as a Metaphor

In the metaphor of the map, your score (from 80 to 400) is like the topography, the depth or height, illustrated on the map. When taken together, the Soulful Capacities allow you to see more *deeply, with more perspective*, and with greater *appreciation for detail*.

The more Acceptance, the more you can see into the moment instead of being afraid of what might arise; the more forgiving the terrain becomes so that you may traverse your path more easily. The more Presence, the deeper you can go into the unfolding occasion; the more attuned you are to the features of the landscape—flowers, rocks, clouds, hills all come more fully into focus. With more Flow, your sense of moment-to-moment change intensifies; your forward motion is heightened; you navigate past obstacles with swift, efficient shifts in motion as they arise, moment to moment. And with Synchronicity, more is revealed about connections between features of the terrain; your senses, like antennae, are sharpened to recognize how the twists and turns of the path, the features of the terrain, and the direction of the wind work together to point the way to your next destination along your journey.

To help with this metaphor, take a look at the images below. At the top is a butterfly. Moving from left to right, the details of the butterfly become clearer. The middle panel shows what appears to be a circle on the left. However, as we move from left to right, the circle gains more dimension, then depth and height, and finally, it appears as an articulated sphere. Finally, the bottom panel shows what appears to be a diamond. As we change perspective, it reveals itself to be a *tesseract* (the four-dimensional analog of the cube; the tesseract is to the cube as the cube is to the square).

These images contain three analogs in our journey of developing greater Soulful Capacity: 1) from blurred vision to seeing with exquisite clarity, 2) from seeing only the surface of things to fully grasping their depth, and 3) from only looking at things from one stationary angle to fully appreciating the dynamics involved from all angles.

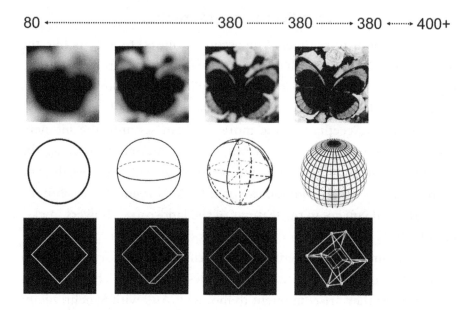

The numbers at the top of the graphic represent the range of the possible scores you received from totaling your results from each of the four self-assessments. Notice that there are three possible "380" scores relative to the images below them. Each of us determines our own level of seeing, of depth, of perspective. The "380" is an arbitrary selection. A "380" (or a "200" or "250" or any score) means something different to me than to you. Again, no judgment.

This is only one source of feedback. You may get feedback from others—a priest, therapist, coach, teacher, or guru. Their guidance may help. When it comes to the journey of your soul, every teacher will ask you to reflect for yourself on where you are in your own journey.

Similarly, note that the "400+" is placed outside (to the far right) of all the images. This placement is meant to convey that the images themselves are limited. A high level of Soulful Capacity (or temporal competency) cannot really be captured by a single number, image, any words, or experience. In developing Soulful Capacity, we are not aspiring. We are not achieving. We are more about being *in and with* time.

From Unfolding to Enfolding

Our soul unfolds through our experience of wholeness and the Soulful Capacities help us to experience the unfolding and the wholeness. Consider these three self-assessment statements from previous sections in this book.

The events in my life unfold according to a divine or greater plan.

I feel in control of the events unfolding in my life.

My life story unfolds in ways that feel like destiny.

In contrast to the soul that unfolds, our personality enfolds. It represents, is made up of, and constitutes the Radiant Forces. I have three different reasons for introducing the essential capacities above and before discussing personality (see Book 3). First, these capacities lie close to the deeper universal forces and are essential to know for your time empowerment. We can over-identify with our personalities. Therefore, we have difficulty seeing deeper natural forces at work as they influence our life and our experience of life. Second, most personality assessments, quizzes, and tools have little to do with the soul. The modern world—with a plethora of personality tests and less emphasis on the soul—makes it difficult to see the limits of personality. Discussions of "what is your type?" can reify or lead to identification with, pride for, and attachment to a measure mindset.

Last, the current science of psychology, even positive psychology, can overemphasize behavior or the *surface* of our intentions, actions, and habits. Science can ignore the spiritual, soulful, or archetypal stirrings that underlie and even cause behaviors, intentions, and our longings for an experience of life's Treasures. For example, one of the most well-known ideas in psychology is expressed in the following formula: "Our behavior is a function of both our personality (internal dispositions or character traits) and the environment or situation we are in."

Almost everything we do is determined by two factors:

✦ how our traits (tendencies, motives, attitudes) get expressed in different ways depending on the environment we are in; and

✦ how different environments pull for, stimulate, evoke or elicit different traits, which then get expressed in behavior.

So, there are three variables in the formula: behavior (B), personality (p), and environment (e). As a formula, it looks like this:

$$B = f\,(p \times e)$$

Behavior (B) is a function (f) of the matching up or interaction (x) between personality and environment. Thousands of research articles in modern psychology have assessed one or more aspects of this formula. In contrast, in this happening life, the focus is more on *experiencing* the Treasures of this happening life than on behavior.

We could restate the above formula: "Our experience of the Treasures in this happening life is a function of both our *Soulful Capacities* and the operation of the *Forces* in the *moments* and *occasions* of our life." In other words, the Soulful Capacities lie behind and give shape to our personality, and the forces lie behind and give shape to the environment. This is expressed as a formula:

$$T = f\,(s \times F)$$

The experience of a Treasure (T) is a function (f) of the matching up or interaction (x) between our soul (s) and the Forces (F). In philosophy and the field of depth psychology, this is also called the relationship between the psyche (our soul and personality) and the cosmos.

Our job in life is one of reconciliation, to find a way to make these two get along, to nourish their marriage. The above formula is a corollary to QfP. Just as the quest is a function of our presence (QfP), our Presence to the Treasures of life (T) emerges as an interplay between our soul and the eternal, cosmological forces.

To review, here are the three reasons for waiting until now to approach personality. First, the Soulful Capacities are often neglected but lie much closer to the forces than personality. Second, it is likely that if you have done any previous personality assessments, they have not involved soulful or spiritual aspects. Finally, modern psychology overemphasizes the outward manifestation of behaviors rather than revealing the deeper forces that inspire them.

Because of these three reasons, I believe it would be misleading to present the personality (the enfoldings) before Soulful Capacities. There is a great temptation to over-identify with personality and under-identify with soul, to get caught up in discussions or ideas about one's personality type or one's score on a test, and to mistakenly focus on the surface of our life and forget the real purpose of our journey.

Tendencies Toward the Four Forces

The Soulful Capacities lie close to or have some correspondence with four radiant and cosmological forces. Knowing these correspondences will help your time empowerment. First, here is a brief review of the forces that were described in detail in QfP Book 1.

Form (also Structure, Organization). Form represents an objective reality that everything has a shape, a recognizable pattern, integrity, or coherence. Our ego often gets attached to form.

Chaos (also Entropy, Dissolution). Chaos represents an objective reality that everything is in a state of disintegration. We glimpse Chaos in experiences of randomness, challenges, disruption, the unknown. Our ego often has an aversion to and avoids chaos.

Time Shaping (or Causality, Action). Time Shaping represents an objective reality where one entity or object has an influence or impact on other entities or the shape of an event or events. We understand Time Shaping through intentionality, desire, or will and subsequent behaviors. Our ego often takes pride in the actions we take and our ability to influence events.

Nurturing Conditions (also Temporal Context, Becoming, Facilitative Conditions, Cooperating Cause). Nurturing Conditions represent an objective reality that everything is in the process of unfolding, of becoming, of coming into being, or transitioning from one form to the next. We glimpse nurturing conditions in *processes*: in experiences of waiting, arriving, growing, decaying. It is through Nurturing Conditions that we understand *timeless* aspects of existence.

There is a tendency for each of the Soulful Capacities to have a unique sensitivity to the four Radiant Forces. These are only tendencies, and they are helpful to know.

✦ **Acceptance** often comes when we need to let go of the moment and allow things to be what they exactly are. Hence, the current *Form* of anything—our life, our relationship, our health—is what is often being called into Acceptance. We perceive and honor the pattern which connects.

✦ **Presence** usually emerges when events and occasions in our life become challenging, turn chaotic, or we experience failure or feel out of control. Hence, *Chaos* in any area of our life encourages us to be present.

✦ **Flow** becomes more important in the midst of taking action, when achieving in performance, or when doing some creative activity. Hence, the more we want to soulfully excel at *Time Shaping*, the more that Flow will come into our lives.

✦ **Synchronicity** arises in our search for connections, for patterns, for meaning; when following our intuition; and when exploring what is possible, what may come forth. Hence, those *Nurturing Conditions* that are behind the coexistence of everything affords Synchronicity in our lives.

As explained in Book 1, the Radiant Forces are always unfolding, in all ways and all the time. Your life journey requires working with these forces. The Soulful Capacities are your resources as a journeyer. They give you the ability to embrace life fully. As you encounter the forces, the capacities grow and mature. Life is a give-and-take between the calling of your soul and the situations you find yourself in.

Over the course of our journey, the forces unfold the meaning of that journey as unique as it is—why specifically we are here—to the degree that our souls are ready to have them unfold. At the same time, these Radiant Forces act within and through us. Our distinct personality is also made up of those same forces. They are *enfolded* within us in a unique pattern, unlike any other pattern that exists in the entire world. Each of us has a unique personal attraction to the path of our own spiritual development.

Book 3 explains the process of enfolding in more detail. For now, it may help to know that your attraction to spiritual growth emerges as you collect, incorporate, and blend information from three sources: the world you live in, inklings and insights that come through the Soulful Capacities, and your experience of Transcendence, Timelessness, and life's Treasures.

Together, the unfolding of life and our stitch by stitch enfolding of information continually create the precious tapestry of the new sense of time at the heart of our quest for presence. At one point in our journey, the weave is the map. At another point, it is the veil. When it comes to our personality, we are both a weave and a veil. But it is a veil of many folds, ones made up of the very substance we are seeking.

The personality—our uniqueness—can be both a blessing and a curse. As a blessing, it is our very uniqueness that allows us to reflect the Radiant Forces outward into the world. Each of us is a blessing to and for others. At the same time, our personality can lead us to take ourselves too seriously and keep us from seeing things as they really are. Personality is always limiting and limited. The best attitude is to:

+ appreciate and value your uniqueness,

+ stay humble and avoid over-identifying with your own uniqueness,

+ view your personality as something that your soul, out of compassion for you, has decided to befriend, and

+ in this friendship, use your personality and soul together to better negotiate with and master the forces.

REFLECTION

Understanding personality only through books and tests can be a deceit. It has been so for me. For the past forty years, I have studied different theories and have taken many personality tests. I both participated in and led retreats designed to realize personality. As a professor, I taught personality studies. My doctoral dissertation involved developing a measure of personality. Different tests assess me as a helper, a catalyst, intense, interdependent, extraverted, and inclined toward "childlike" qualities. I am intuitive with strengths in connectedness and strategy, and I have a high need to influence. These are just examples.

When I taught personality, the students and I would read a biography together at the end of the semester. We would apply theories to understand the individual. During this time, we studied John Lennon, Nelson Mandela, Marilyn Monroe, Jaqueline Kennedy-Onassis, and Pablo Picasso. Then, as now, I felt it important to study the person as a whole and not just an assembly of traits.

Despite study, I felt that my own personality fell apart whenever I had a romantic breakup or encountered failure. Insights from the study of personality did not help. Gaining *Acceptance* first helped me. Being *present* to my own longings and fears and griefs helped me.

The last time I taught, we studied Picasso. During that semester, I was dealing with a romantic breakup and leaving my profession as a college professor. In many ways, I felt that my life was a lie. I was an impostor. Interestingly, Picasso said: "Art is a lie that makes us realize the truth."

This quote may reflect Picasso's own egotistical life, with fractured relationships, family, and abuse of others. He was an artistic genius, but he caused suffering. For me, no amount of "art" or outward work helped me come to terms with my own shortcomings. The hard truth was that my teaching was keeping me from myself. I could hide behind the assessments and theories instead of doing the deeper and inner "soul work."

I am still a work in progress. Over and through time, I have come to know my "self" (my personality) better, by accepting my character defects (e.g., through 12-step work), being more present to my feelings (e.g., through psychotherapy), learning to flow (e.g., through yoga, meditation, and different types of body-work), and being grateful for the many coincidences and synchronicities that make my life rich and meaningful.

A Closing Affirmation

"I am a work in progress" means my soul is working.
I pause to accept this fact, show up with presence to
witness my life, flow as I listen for what comes next,
and find the hidden treasure in every shortcoming
or challenge. I am attracted to my own destiny.

Other Souful Capacities

The four Soulful Capacities are only some of the essential aspects of our humanness. We focus on these four because they seem to have a special relationship to our experience of time. They foster a more holistic and healthy experience beyond the veil of clock-time. The same might be said for those listed below, taken from different traditions and approaches.

Nine Essential Aspects of the Soul through the Enneagram	The Four Paramitas in Buddhist Loving Kindness (Metta) Practice	The Seven Graces (Christianity)
1. Essential Goodness, Sacredness, Integrity	1. Loving Kindness	1. Insight (Prophecy)
2. Essential Love, Sweetness	2. Compassion	2. Helpfulness (Service or Ministry)
3. Essential Value, Glory	3. Sympathetic Joy	3. Instruction (Teaching)
4. Essential Identity, Depth	4. Equanimity	4. Encouragement
5. Essential Clarity, Illumination, Brilliance, Discovery	**The Soul Encouragement of Virtues (Sikhism)**	5. Generosity (Giving)
6. Essential Awakeness, Guidance, Truth	1. Dayā (Compassion)	6. Guidance (Leadership)
7. Essential Freedom, Joy	2. Sat (Integrity, Purity)	7. Compassion (Mercy)
8. Essential Strength, Aliveness	3. Santokh (Contentment)	
9. Essential Wholeness, Unity	4. Nimratā (Humility)	
	5. Prem (Love)	
	6. Khimā (Forgiveness)	
	7. Himmat (Courage)	
	8. Dhīraj (Patient Endurance)	
	9. Chardī Kalā (Positivity)	

The essential aspects of the Enneagram are derived from the original spiritual Enneagram, or Holy Ideas, as developed by Oscar Ichazo and the Arica School. Please refer to www.arica.org

Readers can learn about the first four paramitas (translated as "perfections" or "completeness") from the work of Sharon Salzberg. Please refer to Salzberg, S. (1995). *Lovingkindness: The Revolutionary Art of Happiness*. Shambhala Publications, Inc. Other paramitas in Mahayana Buddhism include (1) generosity (dāna), (2) morality (sīla), (3) renunciation (nekhamma), (4) insight (paññā), (5) energy (viriya), (6) patience (khanti), (7) truthfulness (sacca), and (8) resolution (adhitthāna).

To study more about the nine qualities in Sikhism, please refer to https://www.sikhiwiki.org/.

The Biblical source text for the seven graces is found in the New Testament, Romans 12: 6-8 (NIV).

Key Terms

Acceptance. One of the four Soulful Capacities, Acceptance refers to allowing the moment, the situation, and the conditions of one's life (past, present, future) to be just as they are, without adding anything to it (as in desiring or needing more) or taking anything away from it (as in avoiding, regretting, or denying).

Clock-time. As used in *Quest for Presence*, clock-time refers to the earth-bound use of a physical and mechanical device that is: (1) used to measure time for a social or public group, (2) in order for that group to keep track of time, and (3) as a way to introduce order in reference to the 24-hour day of the earth's rotational cycle. There are other types of clocks, such as a biological clock that refers to biological cycles and a psychological clock that refers to our own internal sense of time. From the perspective of the human species, physical and mechanical clock-time is relative and subjective; it is an idiosyncratic artifice of measuring time because of the earth's axis and rotation in reference to the sun. Clock-time on another planet would be entirely different. In *Quest for Presence*, we attempt to understand clock-time as objectively as possible and without negative judgment. It is sometimes referred to as small "t" time or time on the surface in comparison to a big "T" time, a more comprehensive view of time that is deeper and more important for Presence.

Consciousness. Consciousness is defined here as the actual use of awareness to control attention in reference to space and time, in reference to information that resides in space and time, and in reference to information that emerges as we attend to space and time.

Contemplation. Contemplation is both an action and a thing (for example, a poem, work of art, writing exercise) in *Quest for Presence.* As an action, it occurs when we intentionally look thoughtfully at something for a long time. As a thing, the written contemplations at the end of each chapter are devices or exercises provided to encourage the act of Contemplation.

Flow. One of the four Soulful Capacities, Flow refers to a state in which people are immersed in an activity that is intrinsically enjoyable. This state has several qualities: clear goals, getting immediate feedback from actions, merging actions with awareness, excluding worries and distractions, having a sense of control, and losing a sense of time.

Personality (also outer self, persona, mask). As defined here, personality refers to a set of traits and qualities that distinguishes how a person appears unique or would be characterized as unique by others. Personality is distinct from, and more at the surface, as compared with one's more inner self, essence, or soul.

Presence. One of the four Soulful Capacities, Presence refers to being centered in the moment and the ability to be fully attentive to oneself and one's environment, with a sense of aliveness, full engagement, and tuning in to the moment with heart and mind.

Radiant Forces. The fundamental or deep source of the precious weave and discussed in depth in Book 1. The Forces are specifically forces *of time*; that is, everything that happens and that we experience *as happening* emerges or unfolds through the activity of these forces. Each force is itself energy and strength with the potential to move things, influence, and provide power, ultimately causing our experience to unfold.

Self-Actualization. This term, associated with the work of the psychologist Abraham Maslow, refers to the drive within all human beings to reach one's full potential to achieve a sense of self-fulfillment in one or more areas of life. In this book, self-actualization is distinct from self-transcendence, which Maslow positioned as a higher-order drive.

Self-Transcendence. This term, associated with the work of the psychologist Abraham Maslow, refers to the drive within all human beings to further a cause beyond the self and to experience a communion beyond the boundaries of the self through peak experience. Unlike self-actualization, which seeks to bring out the highest and best potential of one's identity, self-transcendence seeks to go beyond the self to a state of egolessness.

Soul. As defined here, the soul is that inherent aspect of a living being that contains information from the entire universe, is accessible through and animates consciousness, and evolves and unfolds through the experience of connection provided by time and through all past and future incarnations of that aspect of being.

Soulful Capacity. A Soulful Capacity refers to our innate and ever-present ability to experience the precious weave and the operation of the Radiant Forces, especially as those forces manifest in the Treasures of this happening life. The *Quest for Presence* identifies four such capacities: Acceptance, Presence, Flow, and Synchronicity. They are soulful because they come from and help us tap into a more enduring, essential, and transcendent experience of our journey in this life.

Synchronicity. One of the four Soulful Capacities, Synchronicity refers to the experience of two or more events that are apparently causally unrelated or unlikely to occur together by chance, yet are experienced as occurring together in a meaningful manner.

Tao. Tao or Dao is a Chinese word meaning the way, path, route, or road. In Chinese philosophy, Tao is the absolute principle underlying the universe, combining within itself the principles of yin and yang and signifying the way, or code of behavior, that is in harmony with the natural order.

Treasure (see Book 5). A Treasure is an experience—a state of consciousness—wherein one directly witnesses the value or preciousness of life *as it is happening* and in a way that brings a sense of uplift, wholeness, transcendence, insight, intimacy, deep perception, or (usually) some combination of these qualities. In *Quest for Presence*, the Treasures alter our sense of time; we become more present. The Treasures are not "out there" in the future. Treasures occur at the intersection of the Soulful Capacities and the Radiant Forces.

Research Notes

CHAPTER 1

(page 9) **The act of reading itself.** The dual theme of work and play informs Book 2. On one hand, the soul recognizes it is here for a short time and has "holy work" to do: to guide the individual to make a contribution, do good, experience some fulfillment, and love well. On the other hand, the soul is utterly relaxed: it knows its original oneness with the universe, cosmos, God, Being. Here it guides the individual to play, have fun, enjoy leisure, rest, and otherwise abandon any urgency. Our human experience of distinctive qualities of time—and the Treasures—emerges from these two soul-tasks of guiding work and guiding play. It is through and beyond work and play that the soul awakens. The Contemplations in this book, by themselves, will not awaken your soul. They are only prompting your attention to time while you work and play and to work and play *with* time. For more on awakening the soul, I encourage reading the following books:

Meade, M. (2018). *Awakening the soul: A deep response to a troubled world.* GreenFire Press.

Moore, T. (1992). *Care of the soul.* HarperCollins.

Needleman, J. (2003). *Time and the soul: Where has all the meaningful time gone—And can we get it back?* Berrett-Koehler.

(page 9) **Indeed, our mental well-being … technology and the experience of time, reading, and internet use.** There is a wide range of opinion on how and whether reading (for example, a book or magazine) versus using the internet and smartphones influences our experience of time. These references provide compelling ideas as a starting place. I especially like Lupton's thesis that the growth of reading as a leisure activity beginning in the eighteenth century significantly transformed how human beings experience time as a positive resource. Leisure through literature is a gateway to soulful presence.

Carr, N. (2020). *The shallows: What the internet is doing to our brains.* W. W. Norton & Company.

Loan, F. A. (2009, February 10–11). *Impact of new technology on reading habits: A glimpse on the world literature* [Paper presentation]. Role of School Libraries in Quality Education, New Deli, India. http://eprints.rclis.org/20084/1/NCERT.pdf

Lupton, C. (2018). *Reading and the making of time in the eighteenth century*. Johns Hopkins University Press.

(page 12) We step off the mirage of the clock-time treadmill. Philosophers, mystics, and scientists have argued, and also provided evidence, for the idea that clock-time is not real or is purely a function of our biology and perception, a way of creating order in the world. These ideas range from the foundational ideas in the ancient Hindu Bhagavad-Gita, where birth and death are an illusion, to modern-day physics. Albert Einstein wrote, "People like us, who believe in physics, know that the distinction between past, present, and future is only a stubbornly persistent illusion."

Barbour, J. (2000). *The end of time: The next revolution in our understanding of the universe*. Oxford University Press.

Jaffe, A. (2018). The illusion of time. *Nature*, 556, 304–305. https://doi.org/10.1038/D41586-018-04558-7

Mazur, J. (2020). *The clock mirage: Our myth of measured time*. Yale University Press.

Einstein quote from https://Goodreads.com

CHAPTER 2

(page 17) On consciousness during technical death. As with discussions about soul and consciousness, the literature is replete with analyses of near-death experiences (NDEs) and brain function. These range from well-argued studies showing how NDEs provide no proof of the afterlife (Marsh, 2016) and that criticize others who make such claims (Alexander, 2013; van Lommel, 2010). Either way, it appears that the brain subserves the experience of consciousness even when under great duress, that intense experiences (of "presence") can be explained by brain function, and that the intense reality of NDEs appears even more intense than our experience during waking consciousness.

Alexander, E. (2013). *Proof of heaven deluxe edition with dvd: A neurosurgeon's journey into the afterlife*. Simon & Schuster.

Marsh, M. N. (2016). The near-death experience: A reality check? *Humanities*, 5(2), Article 18. https://doi.org/10.3390/h5020018

Mobbs, D., & Watt, C. (2011). There is nothing paranormal about near-death experiences: How neuroscience can explain seeing bright lights, meeting the dead, or being convinced you are one of them. *Trends in Cognitive Sciences*, 15(10), 447–449. https://doi.org/10.1016/j.tics.2011.07.010

Moore, L. E., & Greyson, B. (2017). Characteristics of memories for near-death experiences. *Consciousness and Cognition*, 51, 116–124. https://doi.org/10.1016/j.concog.2017.03.003

van Lommel, P. (2010). *Consciousness beyond life*. HarperOne.

(page 17) The whole of consciousness is more than the sum of its component parts ... theoretical models of consciousness: A scoping review. This review by Sattin and colleagues in the journal *Brain Sciences* is one of the most up-to-date and thorough treatments of this topic. Aside from the different theories and definitions and the other books and articles referenced in this chapter, the work of the neuroscientist Antonio Damasio is important to highlight. For Damasio, consciousness is always embodied in the living being and involves feeling, often feeling about life or that one is alive. Consciousness involves a presence to one's feelings, which live in the body. However, those feelings tell us that we are more than just our bodies (see the next note). The Treasures in QfP, as described in detail in Book 5, are Treasures precisely because they are *feelings* that both highlight and are highlighted by our consciousness of the cosmos that resides within us and also beyond us. Also, the Attractions in QfP, as described in detail in Book 3, produce a feeling (a rising up, quickening, stirring, inkling) in us when we enfold cosmic energies and as we follow our destiny.

Damasio, A. (2021). *Feeling & knowing: Making minds conscious.* Pantheon Books.

Damasio, A. R. (1999). *The feeling of what happens: Body and emotion in the making of consciousness.* Harcourt Brace & Company.

Sattin, D., Magnani, F. G., Bartesaghi, L., Caputo, M., Fittipaldo, A. V., Cacciatore, M., Picozzi, M., & Leonardi, M. (2021). Theoretical models of consciousness: A scoping review. *Brain Sciences, 11*(5), Article 535. https://doi.org/10.3390/brainsci11050535

(page 18) Sebastjan Vörös and neurotheology. The quote is from Vörös, S. (2014). Any number of quotes could convey a similar meaning, as drawn from two fields: the neuroscience of consciousness (for example, Wu, 2018) and neurotheology. Some helpful texts are listed below.

Azari, N. P., Nickel, J., Wunderlich, G., Niedeggen, M., Hefter, H., Tellmann, L., Herzog, H., Stoerig, P., Birnbacher, D., & Seitz, R. J. (2001). Neural correlates of religious experience. *European Journal of Neuroscience, 13*(8), 1649–1652. https://doi.org/10.1046/j.0953-816x.2001.01527.x

McNamara, P. (2009). *The neuroscience of religious experience.* Cambridge University Press.

Newberg, A. B. (2010). *Principles of neurotheology.* Ashgate Publishing.

Vörös, S. (2014). Neurotheologia, quo vadis: Some philosophical problems of neurotheology. *Prolegomena: Časopis za Filozofiju, 13*(2), 351–372. https://hrcak.srce.hr/129632

Wu, W. (2018). The neuroscience of consciousness. In E. N. Zalta (Ed.), *The Stanford Encyclopedia of Philosophy* (Winter 2018 Edition). https://plato.stanford.edu/archives/win2018/entries/consciousness-neuroscience/

(page 19) By almost every definition, the soul is a beautiful thing … on defining the soul. It is, of course, difficult to fully describe and appreciate all the philosophical, spiritual, religious, and even scientific writing about defining the soul. These writings run the gamut from early Egyptian, Hindu, and Greek philosophy to modern skepticism (Cave, 2013). A considerable body of research shows that individuals who have a more analytic mindset are less likely to hold religious beliefs, that atheists and agnostics are more reflective than religious believers, and that non-religious people take more time to reason things out. In developing a model of "this happening life," I attempt to provide a more analytic definition of the soul to show how it functions and to help us more fully experience the Treasures of life. The vast majority of human beings have some idea, concept, or awareness (see next note) that there is *something* (whatever you wish to call it) that exists *outside the duration* of their body and their biological life. This *something* is beyond time. It is not my goal to discuss whether this idea is an opinion, a value, a set of principles, or a spiritual or religious belief, nor whether science (in its current or future evolution) could ever validate the *existence* of the soul. The definition provided here is primarily *functional*. I hope it functions to serve you on your quest. The suggested readings provided below offer a diversity of viewpoints that further attest to the difficult task of deriving a complete definition of soul, which is beyond the scope of this book.

Cave, S. (2013, March 20). What science really says about the soul. *Skeptic*. https://www.skeptic.com/eskeptic/13-03-20/#feature

Daniels, M. (2002). The transpersonal self: 1. A psychohistory and phenomenology of the soul [Preprint Version]. *Transpersonal Psychology Review*, 6(1), 17–28. https://citeseerx.ist.psu.edu/viewdoc/download?doi=10.1.1.589.9844&rep=rep1&type=pdf

Holloway, R. (2016). *A little history of religion*. Yale University Press.

Moore, T. (1992). *Care of the soul*. HarperCollins.

Olafson, F. A. (2019, June 4). Philosophical anthropology. *Encyclopedia Britannica*. https://www.britannica.com/topic/philosophical-anthropology

Pennycook, G., Ross, R. M., Koehler, D. J., & Fugelsang, J. A. (2016). Atheists and agnostics are more reflective than religious believers: Four empirical studies and a meta-analysis. *PLOS ONE*, *11*(4), Article e0153039. https://doi.org/10.1371/journal.pone.0153039

(page 19) Ancient views of the soul. The references below pertain to ideas outside of Ancient Greece and platonic conceptions of the soul.

Amit, N. A. (2013). *Diogenes of Babylon on the soul* (Order No. 28754141) [Doctoral dissertation, University of Haifa]. ProQuest Dissertations & Theses Global.

Asante, M. K. (2014). The idea of the human soul in ancient Egypt. *Gaudium Sciendi*, (6), 43–52. https://doi.org/10.34632/gaudiumsciendi.2014.2728

Gillespie, S. D. (2002). Chapter 4. Body and soul among the Maya: Keeping the spirits in place [Special issue]. *Archeological Papers of the American Anthropological Association*, *11*(1), 67–78. https://doi.org/10.1525/ap3a.2002.11.1.67

Hare, W. L. (1928). The Indian idea of the soul. *The Open Court*, *1928*(12), Article 1. https://opensiuc.lib.siu.edu/ocj/vol1928/iss12/1

Quote by Robert Llewellyn from the movie: Johnson, C. (Director). (2015). *A better life: An exploration of joy & meaning in a world without god* [Motion Picture]. Cosmic Teapot.

(page 20) Most people believe in the soul. See research by Pew Research (2018) and the Roper Poll (Weldon, 2015); polls that show while fewer Americans believe in God, more and more individuals do believe in the afterlife (Twenge et al., 2016). People's belief in religion and the need for religion appear to be strongly linked to their belief in death and fear of death (again, a reference to time and the endurance of our being following death). For example, Bentzen (2021) found (from daily data on Google searches for 95 countries) that the COVID-19 crisis has increased Google searches for prayer (relative to all Google searches) to the highest level ever recorded.

Bentzen, J. S. (2021). In crisis, we pray: Religiosity and the COVID-19 pandemic. *Journal of Economic Behavior & Organization, 192,* 541–583. https://doi.org/10.1016/j.jebo.2021.10.014

Pew Research Center (2018, May 29). *Being Christian in western Europe.* http://assets.pewresearch.org/wp-content/uploads/sites/11/2018/05/14165352/Being-Christian-in-Western-Europe-FOR-WEB1.pdf

Twenge, J. M., Sherman, R. A., Exline, J. J., & Grubbs, J. B. (2016). Declines in American adults' religious participation and beliefs, 1972–2014. *SAGE Open, 6*(1). https://doi.org/10.1177/2158244016638133

Weldon, K. (2015, June 15). *Paradise polled: Americans and the afterlife.* HuffPost. https://www.huffingtonpost.com/kathleen-weldon/paradise-polled-americans_b_7587538.html

(pages 20–21) A sample of definitions…diverse definitions of soul. A full modern analysis of soul would take volumes to represent. Those mentioned here are a diverse sampling. The writings of A. H. Almaas can be accessed through www.diamondapproach.org. One page provides multiple excerpts on the definition of essence (see "Personal Essence" in Glossary), many drawn from his 1988 book, *The Pearl Beyond Price,* Diamond Books. Ken Wilber's work can be found on the website https://integrallife.com/. A good starting place is his 1979 book, *No Boundary: Eastern and Western Approaches to Personal Growth* (now from Shambala Publications). Also consider the work of Gary Zukav (The Seat of the Soul) and https://seatofthesoul.com/; and also Thomas Moore (Care of the Soul) and https://www.thomasmooresoul.com/

(page 21) Abraham Maslow and research on self-transcendence. The study of self-transcendence as a psychological construct cuts across diverse areas of interest. This includes its measurement, its role in transcendent experiences, its importance in life stories, and its potential role in neuropsychological function.

Garcia-Romeu, A. (2010). Self-transcendence as a measurable transpersonal construct. *The Journal of Transpersonal Psychology, 42*(1), 26–47. https://www.atpweb.org/jtparchive/trps-42-10-01-026.pdf

Johnstone, B., Hanks, R., Bhushan, B., Cohen, D., Roseberry, J., & Yoon, D. P. (2017). Selflessness as a universal neuropsychological foundation of spiritual transcendence: Validation with Christian, Hindu, and Muslim traditions. *Mental Health, Religion & Culture, 20*(2), 175–187. https://doi.org/10.1080/13674676.2017.1333090

Reischer, H. N., Roth, L. J., Villarreal, J. A., & McAdams, D. P. (2021). Self-transcendence and life stories of humanistic growth among late-midlife adults. *Journal of Personality, 89*(2), 305–324. https://doi.org/10.1111/jopy.12583

Yaden, D. B., Haidt, J., Hood, R. W., Jr., Vago, D. R., & Newberg, A. B. (2017). The varieties of self-transcendent experience. *Review of General Psychology, 21*(2), 143–160. https://doi.org/10.1037/gpr0000102

(page 22) On soul and consciousness. The study of the relationship between human consciousness and the soul is even more complex than the study of defining either of them. I particularly suggest Julian Jaynes's work. I had the privilege of hearing Jaynes lecture on the bicameral mind. *Bicameralism* is the idea that human beings have evolved from having a brain that did not distinguish between aspects that were linguistic or speaking and aspects that were auditory or hearing. About 3,000 years ago, the ability to have meta-awareness and introspection evolved when humans could take their own thoughts as content or subject to attend to. That is, there was a time when human beings could not perceive, let alone label, their own thoughts as subjects in and of themselves. This ability to use words for reflecting on one's own mind is seen as the birth of consciousness and also the idea that there is a soul that continues on in time after we are here (and have the ability to label it). The following references provide a rich array of thoughtful insights and show that there is no consensus on the definition of consciousness and much less on the relationship consciousness has with the soul. For a general review of definitions, I suggest *The Stanford Encyclopedia of Philosophy* (Van Gulick, 2018).

Bładek, I., Komosinski, M., & Miazga, K. (2019). Mappism: Formalizing classical and artificial life views on mind and consciousness. *Foundations of Computing and Decision Sciences, 44*(1), 55–99. https://doi.org/10.2478/fcds-2019-0005

Crick, F. (1995). *The astonishing hypothesis: The scientific search for the soul.* Simon & Schuster.

Ginsburg, S., & Jablonka, E. (2019). *The evolution of the sensitive soul: Learning and the origins of consciousness.* The MIT Press.

Grandy, J. K. (2018). The three neurogenetic phases of human consciousness. *Journal of Conscious Evolution, 9*(9), Article 4. https://digitalcommons.ciis.edu/cejournal/vol9/iss9/4

Jaynes, J. (2000). *The origin of consciousness in the breakdown of the bicameral mind.* Houghton Mifflin Harcourt.

Lorenz, H. (2003). Ancient theories of soul. In E. N. Zalta (Ed.), *The Stanford Encyclopedia of Philosophy* (Winter 2003 Edition). https://plato.stanford.edu/entries/ancient-soul/

Pereira, C., & Reddy, J. S. K. (2016). Near-death cases desegregating non-locality/disembodiment via quantum mediated consciousness: An extended version of the cell-soul pathway. *Journal of Consciousness Exploration & Research, 7*(11), 951–968. https://core.ac.uk/download/pdf/80762466.pdf

Van Gulick, R. (2018). Consciousness. In E. N. Zalta (Ed.), *The Stanford Encyclopedia of Philosophy* (Spring 2018 Edition). https://plato.stanford.edu/archives/spr2018/entries/consciousness/

Wiese, W. (2018). Toward a mature science of consciousness. *Frontiers in Psychology, 9*, Article 693. https://doi.org/10.3389/fpsyg.2018.00693

(page 22) A modern definition … neuroscience and daily spiritual experience. Many modern authors, mostly through philosophical speculation, espouse the relationship between brain and nervous system activity and spiritual experience. Interested readers might search the term *neurotheology*. My double majors as an undergraduate were in philosophy and psychology with a focus on neurotheology. The idea of the universe as a hologram, which is represented in our brain functioning like a hologram, has its origins in the work of the cosmologist David Bohm and the neuroscientist Karl Pribram and, more recently, in the Human Connectome Project (Van Essen et al., 2013). The cosmologist Jude Currivan also helps to build bridges between modern physics and the holographic model. References below provide some touchpoints for further investigation. Clearly, more studies are needed to tie together measures of spiritual experience (e.g., Underwood et al., 2002; Storie & Vining, 2018), with analysis of brain functioning (e.g., Fingelkurts & Fingelkurts, 2009).

Currivan, J. (2017). *The cosmic hologram: In-formation at the center of creation.* Inner Traditions. Also see http://www.judecurrivan.com/

Fingelkurts, A. A., & Fingelkurts, A. A. (2009). Is our brain hardwired to produce God, or is our brain hardwired to perceive God? A systematic review on the role of the brain in mediating religious experience. *Cognitive Processing, 10,* 293–326. https://doi.org/10.1007/s10339-009-0261-3

Gleiser, M. (2017, April 5). *Is neuroscience rediscovering the soul?* NPR. https://www.npr.org/sections/13.7/2017/04/05/522738015/is-neuroscience-rediscovering-the-soul

Kesserwani, H. (2020). An analytic dissection of a case of cerebral diplopia: Is the human brain a holographic device? *Cureus, 12*(9), e10292. https://doi.org/10.7759/cureus.10292

Nichol, L. (Ed.). *The essential David Bohm.* Routledge.

Pribram, K. H. (2013). *The form within: My point of view.* Prospecta Press.

Storie, M., & Vining, J. (2018). From oh to aha: Characteristics and types of environmental epiphany experiences. *Human Ecology Review, 24*(1), 155–180. https://doi.org/10.22459/HER.24.01.2018.08

Underwood, L. G., & Teresi, J. A. (2002). The daily spiritual experience scale: Development, theoretical description, reliability, exploratory factor analysis, and preliminary construct validity using health-related data. *Annals of Behavioral Medicine, 24*(1), 22–33. https://doi.org/10.1207/s15324796abm2401_04

Van Essen, D. C., Smith, S. M., Barch, D. M., Behrens, T. E. J., Yacoub, E., & Ugurbil, K. (2013). The WU-Minn human connectome project: An overview. *NeuroImage, 80,* 62–79. https://doi.org/10.1016/j.neuroimage.2013.05.041

(page 23) Varieties of spiritual experience. The classic text in this area of research was the American psychologist William James's *The Varieties of Religious Experience* (originally published in 1902). Other examples are provided below.

Berkovich-Ohana, A., & Glicksohn, J. (2017). Meditation, absorption, transcendent experience, and affect: Tying it all together via the consciousness state space (CSS) model. *Mindfulness, 8.* 68–77. https://doi.org/10.1007/s12671-015-0481-9

Garcia-Romeu, A., Himelstein, S. P., & Kaminker, J. (2014). Self-transcendent experience: A grounded theory study. *Qualitative Research, 15*(5), 633–654. https://doi.org/10.1177/1468794114550679

James, W. (2008). *The varieties of religious experience: A study in human nature*. Routledge.

Yaden, D. B., Haidt, J., Hood, R. W., Jr., Vago, D. R., & Newberg, A. B. (2017). The varieties of self-transcendent experience. *Review of General Psychology, 21*(2), 143–160. https://doi.org/10.1037/gpr0000102

Yaden, D. B., Iwry, J., Slack, K. J., Eichstaedt, J. C., Zhao, Y., Vaillant, G. E., & Newberg, A. B. (2016). The overview effect: Awe and self-transcendent experience in space flight. *Psychology of Consciousness: Theory, Research, and Practice, 3*(1), 1–11. https://doi.org/10.1037/cns0000086

(page 24) For research on measures of gratitude. The study of gratitude has increased significantly in the past ten years. Most recently, there have been two meta-analyses showing how gratitude interventions improve health and mental well-being (Boggiss et al., 2020; Cregg et al., 2021).

Boggiss, A. L., Consedine, N. S., Brenton-Peters, J. M., Hofman, P. L., & Serlachius, A. S. (2020). A systematic review of gratitude interventions: Effects on physical health and health behaviors. *Journal of Psychosomatic Research, 135*, Article 110165. https://doi.org/10.1016/j.jpsychores.2020.110165

Cregg, D. R., & Cheavens, J. S. (2021). Gratitude interventions: Effective self-help? A meta-analysis of the impact on symptoms of depression and anxiety. *Journal of Happiness Studies, 22*(1), 413–445. https://doi.org/10.1007/s10902-020-00236-6

Salsman, J. M., Lai, J. S., Hendrie, H. C., Butt, Z., Zill, N., Pilkonis, P. A., Peterson, C., Stoney, C. M., Brouwers, P., & Cella, D. (2014). Assessing psychological well-being: Self-report instruments for the NIH Toolbox. *Quality of Life Research, 23*(1), 205–215. https://doi.org/10.1007/s11136-013-0452-3

Wood, A. M., Froh, J. J., & Geraghty, A. W. A. (2010). Gratitude and well-being: A review and theoretical integration. *Clinical Psychology Review, 30*(7), 890–905. https://doi.org/10.1016/j.cpr.2010.03.005

Also, the National Institutes of Health in the U.S. has an initiative to develop a measurement toolbox for assessing positive life attributes. https://neuroscienceblueprint.nih.gov/resources-tools/blueprint-resources-tools-library/nih-toolbox-assessment-neurological-and

(page 26) They are not just mental states … mental states or soul? The fact that the Soulful Capacities have temporal qualities makes them subject to empirical study (as in studies of gratitude reviewed in the previous note), rather than those that are "atemporal," existing outside of time and in eternity; and ineffable. The discussion of temporality and atemporality is beyond the purpose of this book. However, several notes below suggest that each of the Soulful Capacities can be quantified and studied. I choose to define them as "soulful" capacities rather than mental states because: (1) they entail the experience of *something* beyond mundane perceptions of time; and (2) they are one feature of the *QfP*, along with the Four cosmic Radiant Forces, that operate independently of us (Book 1). If these were only mental states, we might be misled to limit the purpose of our journey to only achieving these states. The journey is not one of achievement but of unfolding.

CHAPTER 3

(page 31) "Tát Tvam Ási" (Sanskrit) is a phrase from Hinduism and Vedic philosophy, translated variously as "Thou art that," "That thou art," "That art thou" or "You are that," and "All is that." It conveys the intrinsic relationship between the individual and the entire absolute universe. I encourage readers to listen to a song from the American Rock group, The Beach Boys, "All This Is That" from their 1972 album *Carl and the Passions*. "Jai Guru Deva" (Sanskrit) is adapted from Hinduism and translates as "I give thanks to, honor, and praise the heavenly teacher." It is worth listening to a song from the British rock group, The Beatles, "Across the Universe," from their 1970 album *Let It Be*.

(page 32) **Self-acceptance can be cultivated** with a loving and caring family member, friend, life coach, or therapist. While Carl Rogers applied acceptance in client-centered therapy practice, the quantitative study of self-acceptance also occurs within the fields of Rational-Emotive Therapy, Mindfulness, and Acceptance and Commitment Therapy. One of the most up-to-date books on these subjects is by Bernard, M. E. (Ed.) (2014). *The strength of self-acceptance: Theory, practice and research*. Springer Science & Business Media. Acceptance and Commitment Therapy is an evolving and entire set of practices that also effectively promote acceptance. Also, the *Unconditional Self-Acceptance Questionnaire* includes items that are reflected in the self-assessment used in this section.

Beattie, M. (2009). *The language of letting go: Daily meditations on codependency*. Simon & Schuster.

Berger, E. M. (1952). The relation between expressed acceptance of self and expressed acceptance of others. *The Journal of Abnormal and Social Psychology*, 47(4), 778–782. https://doi.org/10.1037/h0061311

Borysenko, J. Z. (2009). *It's not the end of the world: Developing resilience in times of change*. Hay House.

Carson, S. H., & Langer, E. J. (2006). Mindfulness and self-acceptance. *Journal of Rational-Emotive & Cognitive-Behavior Therapy*, 24(1), 29–43. https://doi.org/10.1007/s10942-006-0022-5

Flett, G. L., Besser, A., Davis, R. A., & Hewitt, P. L. (2003). Dimensions of perfectionism, unconditional self-acceptance, and depression. *Journal of Rational-Emotive & Cognitive-Behavior Therapy*, 21(2), 119–138. https://doi.org/10.1023/A:1025051431957

Niebuhr, R. (n.d.). *Serenity prayer*. Beliefnet. Retrieved December 13, 2021 from https://www.beliefnet.com/prayers/protestant/addiction/serenity-prayer.aspx

Tart, C. T. (1987). *Waking up: Overcoming the obstacles to human potential*. Shambhala.

Thompson, B. L., & Waltz, J. A. (2008). Mindfulness, self-esteem, and unconditional self-acceptance. *Journal of Rational-Emotive & Cognitive-Behavior Therapy*, 26(2), 119–126. https://doi.org/10.1007/s10942-007-0059-0

Yadavaia, J. E., Hayes, S. C., & Vilardaga, R. (2014). Using acceptance and commitment therapy to increase self-compassion: A randomized controlled trial. *Journal of Contextual Behavioral Science, 3*(4), 248–257. https://doi.org/10.1016/j.jcbs.2014.09.002

Quotations in this chapter:

Anderson, R. C. (1993). *Some days you're the pigeon ... some days you're the statue.* The Humor Project.

Other quotations in this chapter from Rumi, Art Buchwald, Lao Tzu, and Maya Angelou are from https://Goodreads.com.

Psalm 19:4 from *New King James Version Bible.* (2004). Thomas Nelson Publishers (Original work published in 1982).

(page 38) The *Quest for Presence Inventory*™ contains two main sections: the Soulful Capacities (presented here in *QfP Book 2*) and the Attractions (presented in *QfP Book 3*). The *Quest for Presence Contemplations Workbook* combines both parts for readers who want to take them together and contains additional contemplations for combining and aligning them.

CHAPTER 4

(page 46) Empirical study of presence. The study of Presence in the research literature falls into four camps: Presence in holistic nursing, or therapeutic presence; Presence in the virtual environment of real-world simulations (virtual reality or VR); Presence in spirituality; and Presence through psychological absorption in experience. *Therapeutic presence* means being available with the entirety of one's unique individual being (Paterson & Zderad, 1976) as the "gift of self" (Easter, 2000). One paper (Schubert et al., 2001) assessed multiple dimensions of presence in VR experience and includes sense of immersion, explorations (ability to get up close and examine), involvement (feeling connected to and captivated by the environment), spatial presence (a feeling of being there), and realness. See references below.

Chen, S. K., & Mongrain, M. (2020). Awe and the interconnected self. *The Journal of Positive Psychology, 16*(6), 770–778. https://doi.org/10.1080/17439760.2020.1818808

Easter, A. (2000). Construct analysis of four modes of being present. *Journal of Holistic Nursing, 18*(4), 362–377. https://doi.org/10.1177/089801010001800407

Grassini, S., & Laumann, K. (2020). Questionnaire measures and physiological correlates of presence: A systematic review. *Frontiers in Psychology, 11,* Article 349. https://doi.org/10.3389/fpsyg.2020.00349

Paterson, J. G., & Zderad, L. T. (1976). *Humanistic nursing.* Wiley.

Schubert, T., Friedmann, F., & Regenbrecht, H. (2001). The experience of presence: Factor analytic insights. *Presence: Teleoperators & Virtual Environments, 10*(3), 266–281. https://doi.org/10.1162/105474601300343603

Steere, D. A. (1997). *Spiritual presence in psychotherapy: A guide for caregivers.* Brunner-Routledge.

Steffen, E., & Coyle, A. (2010). Can "sense of presence" experiences in bereavement be conceptualised as spiritual phenomena? *Mental Health, Religion & Culture, 13*(3), 273–291. https://doi.org/10.1080/13674670903357844

(page 49) Quote from George Carlin.

Cohan, N. (Host). (2008, June 23). *Keep 'em separated: Remembering George Carlin* [Audio podcast episode]. In *Talk of the Nation: Obituaries.* NPR. https://www.npr.org/transcripts/91812984

(page 51) The origin of presence exercises. The exercises developed for Presence are adapted from two source texts. Puran and Susanna Bair have created an incredible set of visualization exercises for imagining the heart in multiple dimensions using a technique called "Heart Rhythm Meditation." I want to thank my friend Molly McCormick for introducing this tool into my life. The Bairs have many videos available that can be explored at the Institute for Applied Meditation on the Heart (https://www.iamheart.org/). Also, the work of Richard Strozzi-Heckler, founder of the Strozzi Institute (https://strozziinstitute.com/), contains in-depth exercises for Presence, many stemming from the martial arts and aikido.

Bair, P., & Bair, S. (2007). *Energize your heart in four dimensions.* Living Heart Media.

Strozzi-Heckler, R. (1993). *The anatomy of change: A way to move through life's transitions* (2nd ed.). North Atlantic Books.

Quotations in this chapter:

Ingram, C. (2004). *Passionate presence: Experiencing the seven qualities of awakened awareness.* Gotham Books.

Katie, B. (n.d.) *The work 101.* The Work of Byron Katie. Retrieved December 13, 2021, from https://bit.ly/3FPJDPs

Kidd, S. M. (2007). *Firstlight: The early inspirational writings.* Penguin Books.

Tolle, E. (2004). *The power of now: A guide to spiritual enlightenment.* Namaste Publishing; New World Library.

Wiederkehr, M. (2009). *A tree full of angels: Seeing the holy in the ordinary.* HarperOne.

Other quotations in this chapter from A. A. Milne, Martha Graham, and Pema Chödrön are from https://Goodreads.com.

Quotations in this chapter from George Matthew Adams are from https://BrainyQuote.com.

(page 65) **Empirical study of flow.** This entire section is significantly informed by the following original references and texts from Csikszentmihalyi (1990) and Jackson (1996, 2002). In addition, a recent meta-analysis by Hancock and colleagues (2019) clearly demonstrates the relationship between flow and the "transformation of time" or how perceptions of time are distorted to either speed up or slow down. This includes experiences that "time passes differently" or that one's experience of time and actual measurement of time diverge. A key aspect of Flow and time distortion is the "autotelic" process: "The mark of the autotelic personality is the ability to manage a rewarding balance between the 'play' of challenge finding and the 'work' of skill building" (Csikszentmihalyi, 1990, p. 80).

Csikszentmihalyi, M. (1990). *Flow: The psychology of optimal experience.* Harper & Row.

Engeser, S. (Ed.). (2012). *Advances in flow research.* Springer. https://doi.org/10.1007/978-1-4614-2359-1

Hancock, P. A., Kaplan, A. D., Cruit, J. K., Hancock, G. M., MacArthur, K. R., & Szalma, J. L. (2019). A meta-analysis of flow effects and the perception of time. *Acta Psychologica, 198,* Article 102836. https://doi.org/10.1016/j.actpsy.2019.04.007

Jackson, S. A., & Eklund, R. C. (2002). Assessing flow in physical activity: The flow state scale-2 and dispositional flow scale-2. *Journal of Sport and Exercise Psychology, 24*(2), 133–150. https://doi.org/10.1123/jsep.24.2.133

Jackson, S. A., & Marsh, H. W. (1996). Development and validation of a scale to measure optimal experience: The flow state scale. *Journal of Sport and Exercise Psychology, 18*(1), 17–35. https://doi.org/10.1123/jsep.18.1.17

(page 66) **One Study of Elderly People.** The original study by Baum and colleagues (1984) is only one of many research studies on the relationship between aging and time perception. While the notion that "time passes more quickly as one ages" has some support, there are many nuances in this research field.

Baum, S. K., Boxley, R. L., & Sokolowski, M. (1984). Time perception and psychological well-being in the elderly. *Psychiatric Quarterly, 56*(1), 54–61. https://doi.org/10.1007/BF01324632

Block, R. A., Zakay, D., & Hancock, P. A. (1998). Human aging and duration judgments: A meta-analytic review. *Psychology and Aging, 13*(4), 584–596. https://doi.org/10.1037/0882-7974.13.4.584

Wittmann, M., & Lehnhoff, S. (2005). Age effects in perception of time. *Psychological Reports, 97*(3), 921–935. https://doi.org/10.2466/pr0.97.3.921-935

(page 67) **Eric Erikson.** Eric Erikson (1902–1994) was an important contributor to the field of developmental psychology primarily because of his theory that human beings develop in their psychological maturity across particular stages of growth. He may be most famous for coining the phrase *identity crisis,* but his theory has contributed to significant scientific research across all stages of life. Some key readings from Erikson are listed below. Taking time and doing exercises for a review of one's own life and life transitions is one of the applications of Erikson's work (e.g., Haber, 2006). The ability to flow through life's transitions (from stage to stage) is discussed in *QfP Book 4* in a chapter on Transitions. See Feiler (2020).

Chittister, J. (2013). *For everything a season*. Orbis Books.

Erikson, E. H. (1977). *Life history and the historical moment: Diverse presentations*. W. W. Norton & Company.

Erikson, E. H., & Erikson, J. M. (1998). *The life cycle completed (extended version)*. W. W. Norton & Company.

Feiler, B. (2020). *Life is in the transitions: Mastering change at any age*. Penguin Press.

Gibson, F. (Ed.). (2018). *International perspectives on reminiscence, life review and life story work*. Jessica Kingsley Publishers.

Haber, D. (2006). Life review: Implementation, theory, research, and therapy. *The International Journal of Aging and Human Development, 63*(2), 153–171. https://doi.org/10.2190/DA9G-RHK5-N9JP-T6CC

Quotations in this chapter from Lao Tzu and Alan Wilson Watts are from https://Goodreads.com.

Quotation in this chapter from St. Teresa of Avila is from https://BrainyQuote.com.

Quotation in this chapter from Martin Luther King, Jr. is from https://www.spiritualityandpractice.com/.

CHAPTER 6

(page 84) Meaningful coincidences are not the result of chance. We not only detect coincidences, there are factors that lead us to detect them. See these research studies.

Coleman, S. L., & Beitman, B. D. (2009a). Characterizing high-frequency coincidence detectors. *Psychiatric Annals, 39*(5), 271–279. https://doi.org/10.3928/00485713-20090423-01

Coleman, S. L., Beitman, B. D, & Celebi, E. (2009b). Weird coincidences commonly occur. *Psychiatric Annals, 39*(5), 265–270. https://doi.org/10.3928/00485713-20090421-03

Costin, G., Dzara, K., & Resch, D. (2011). Synchronicity: Coincidence detection and meaningful life events. *Psychiatric Annals, 41*(12), 572–575. https://doi.org/10.3928/00485713-20111104-04

(page 84) A number of authors claim that we can develop this capacity for synchronicity or serendipity ... toward a science of synchronicity. There are at least four (quite disparate) areas of research related to Synchronicity. First, those from analytical psychology of Carl Jung. Up until recently, most writings have been qualitative case studies that follow up from the seminal and classic work of Carl Jung (2010, originally published in 1960). Roderick Main has written several books that follow an analytic path similar to Jung. Second, others suggest that we can cultivate the ability to detect and manifest meaningful coincidences (e.g., Hopcke, 1997; Luna, 2021). Third, serendipity is something experienced as people search information on the internet or in library research (*information studies,* e.g., Erdelez et al. (2016); Foster et al. (2003); Foster & Ellis (2014); Björneborn (2004)). Finally, the field of modern physics—especially the phenomenon of quantum entanglement—suggests explanations for synchronistic experiences.

Björneborn, L. (2004). *Small-world link structures across an academic web space: A library and information science approach* [Doctoral dissertation, Royal School of Library and Information Science]. Researchgate.net. https://www.researchgate.net/publication/200110955_Small-World_Link_Structures_across_an_Academic_Web_Space_A_Library_and_Information_Science_Approach

Browne, L. (2017). *The many faces of coincidence.* Imprint Academic.

Brussat, F., & Brussat, M. A. (n.d.) *Synchronicity.* Spirituality & Practice: Resources for Spiritual Journeys. https://www.spiritualityandpractice.com/explorations/topics/view/10/synchronicity

Cassirer, E. (1944) *An essay on man: An introduction to the philosophy of human culture.* Yale University Press.

Chelsom, P. (Director). (2001). *Serendipity* [Film]. Tapestry Films.

Erdelez, S., Heinström, J., Makri, S., Björneborn, L., Beheshti, J., Toms, E., & Agarwal, N. K. (2016). Research perspectives on serendipity and information encountering. *Proceedings of the Association for Information Science and Technology, 53*(1), 1–5. https://doi.org/10.1002/pra2.2016.14505301011

Foster, A., & Ford, N. (2003). Serendipity and information seeking: An empirical study. *Journal of Documentation, 59*(3), 321–340. https://doi.org/10.1108/00220410310472518

Foster, A. E., & Ellis, D. (2014). Serendipity and its study. *Journal of Documentation, 70*(6), 1015–1038. https://doi.org/10.1108/JD-03-2014-0053

Hopcke, R. H. (1997). *There are no accidents: Synchronicity and the story of our lives.* Riverhead Books.

Jung, C. G. (2010). *Synchronicity: An acausal connecting principle.* Princeton University Press.

Kennedy, P. (2016, January 2). How to cultivate the art of serendipity. *The New York Times (Sunday Opinion).* https://www.nytimes.com/2016/01/03/opinion/how-to-cultivate-the-art-of-serendipity.html

Luna, A. (2021, August 3). *Synchronicity: 7 ways to interpret and manifest it.* Lonerwolf. https://lonerwolf.com/synchronicity/

Main, R. (2004). *The rupture of time: Synchronicity and Jung's critique of modern western culture.* Routledge.

Main, R. (2007). *Revelations of chance: Synchronicity as spiritual experience.* State University of New York Press.

Martin, F., Carminati, F., & Carminati, G. G. (2009). Synchronicity, quantum information and the psyche. *Journal of Cosmology, 3,* 580–589. http://cosmology.com/QuantumConsciousness103.html

Pearson, C. L. (2002). *Consider the butterfly: Transforming your life through meaningful coincidence*. Gibbs Smith.

van Andel, P. (1992). Serendipity: "Expect also the unexpected". *Creativity and Innovation Management, 1*(1), 20–32. https://doi.org/10.1111/j.1467-8691.1992.tb00018.x

von Lucadou, W., Römer, H., & Walach, H. (2007). Synchronistic phenomena as entanglement correlations in generalized quantum theory. *Journal of Consciousness Studies, 14*(4), 50–74. http://www.patriziotressoldi.it/cmssimpled/uploads/includes/QuantumLocadou07.pdf

See this recorded TedX lecture by Pek van Andel on YouTube (Serendipitology | Pek van Andel | TEDxLeuven). https://www.youtube.com/watch?v=r9hUiU2r8nY

(pages 85–86). **You have a special set of antennae for seeing the "pattern that connects" things in nature.** The phrase "pattern that connects" is from Gregory Bateson, a social scientist, ecologist, philosopher, and systems thinker. I had the fortune of hearing Bateson lecture from his book *Steps to an Ecology of Mind* in the 1970s. From my understanding, there are three basic principles behind "the pattern which connects" ideas. First, that nature (in and of itself) and how people think about nature are very different from each other. Second, nature (the biosphere and all ecological systems, including humans) is made up of and defined by deeply interconnected circuits and systems that have an inherent pattern of connection. This may be called ecological interrelatedness, holism, or coherent system dynamics. Finally, human beings have the ability to see these deeper, unitary patterns and aesthetics (the nature and appreciation of beauty). Bateson refers to this as seeing "the pattern which connects."

Bateson, G. (1972). *Steps to an ecology of mind*. Jason Aronson.

Bateson, G. (1978). The pattern which connects. *The CoEvolution Quarterly No. 18 (Summer)*, 5–15.

Harries-Jones, P. (1995). *A recursive vision: Ecological understanding and Gregory Bateson*. University of Toronto Press.

Quotations in this chapter from Rumi, Antero Alli, Louis Pasteur, William Blake, Lisa See, and Nancy Thayer are from https://Goodreads.com.

Quotation in this chapter from William Temple is from https://BrainyQuote.com.

Quote from 2001 movie *Serendipity* (Writer: Marc Klein) Chelsom, P. (Director). (2001). *Serendipity* [Film]. Tapestry Films.

CHAPTER 7

(page 107) **The Enneagram and Dr. Joseph Howell.** As noted, there are many aspects in the teaching of the Enneagram, some of which focus more on the Enneagram of the Holy Ideas or more spiritual aspects that pertain to the essence and soulful qualities (also see "Other Soulful Capacities" on page 149 of this book). Dr. Joseph Howell's podcast *The Real Enneagram* can be accessed through Apple podcasts:

https://podcasts.apple.com/us/podcast/the-real-enneagram/id1447675069. Episodes 56 and 57 (from April 7 and 9, 2020) discuss "The Essential Aspects of the Soul." To my knowledge, the most direct, pure, and immersive experience of the Enneagram can be found through the Arica School (https://www.arica.org/). Recommended readings are below.

Almaas, A. H. (2000). *Facets of unity: The Enneagram of holy ideas.* Shambhala Publications.

Howell, J. B. (2012). *Becoming conscious: The Enneagram's forgotten passageway.* Balboa Press.

Maitri, S. (2000). *The spiritual dimension of the Enneagram: Nine faces of the soul.* Jeremy P. Tarcher/Putnam.

(page 109). Modern psychology divorced itself from spiritual matters ... the evolution of the soul in modern psychological science. Modern empirical science, focusing only on what can be measured, has different branches that have progressively avoided discussions of the soul. The first Research Note in Chapter 9 below (*Items that measure spiritual health and self-transcendence*) provides diverse references to the study of self-transcendence and spiritual health. But even these measures make only incidental reference to the "soul." The paper by Koltko-Rivera (2006) argues that Maslow's model of human needs placed "self-actualization" rather than "self-transcendence" at the top of the pyramid because the topic was taboo and outside the social norms of science. Three different subfields within academic psychology touch on these experiences. Still today, it is the least popular or recognized subfield that is the most open to talk of the soul. This is the field of transpersonal psychology founded by Maslow, which has several research journals (including the *Journal of Transpersonal Psychology*) and associations (see http://www.atpweb.org/). A related field is humanistic psychology, which also has research journals and an academic association (https://ahpweb.org/). However, the field that has grown the most in the past twenty years makes the least reference to the soul. According to the *Journal of Positive Psychology*, positive psychology "is about scientifically informed perspectives on what makes life worth living, focusing on aspects of the human condition that lead to happiness, fulfillment, and flourishing." Topics of study include awe, joy, altruism, flow, happiness, hope, optimism, positive thinking, and mindfulness. All good stuff. Yet, the theories or explanations of these phenomena are almost completely temporal and make no reference to the soul.

Koltko-Rivera, M. E. (2006). Rediscovering the later version of Maslow's hierarchy of needs: Self-transcendence and opportunities for theory, research, and unification. *Review of General Psychology, 10*(4), 302–317. https://doi.org/10.1037/1089-2680.10.4.302

Quotations in this chapter:

Bhagavad Gita 3:27, 14:5 from https://www.holy-bhagavad-gita.org

Bible Quote from *New International Version Bible.* (2011). Zondervan

Matthew 10:14, 26 from the *Holy Bible, New International Version,* https://biblehub.com/

CHAPTER 8

(**pages 113–114**). **Interpretations of the Í Ching.** This is just one interpretation of the Hexagram on Contemplation. There are many. Another example from Huang (1998, 2010) is provided below for comparison and because the process of Contemplation is so central in our *Quest for Presence*.

Watching the divine Tao of Heaven, / The four seasons proceed without error

Huang, A. (1998, 2010). *The complete I Ching* (A. Huang, Trans.). Inner Traditions.

Wilhelm, R., Trans. (1950). *The I Ching or Book of Changes* (C. F. Baynes, Trans.). Bollingen Series XIX; Pantheon Books.

Xi, F. (2015). *I Ching: The Book of Change: A new translation.* (Hinton, D., Trans.). Macmillan.

CHAPTER 9

(**pages 119–120**). **Your Personal Quest: Items that measure spiritual health and self-transcendence.** Here are the references to the different items sampled in this chapter. I provide these here as a jumping-off place for readers interested in the two lines of research—spiritual health and self-transcendence—and for further studies that examine their similarities and differences.

Item 1: Spiritual Well-Being Scale (FACIT-Sp)—for example, see Canada, A. L., Murphy, P. E., Fitchett, G., Peterman, A. H., & Schover, L. R. (2008). A 3-factor model for the FACIT-Sp. *Psycho-Oncology*, 17(9), 908–916. https://doi.org/10.1002/pon.1307

Item 2: Advocate HealthCare's Health Risk Assessment—Page 10 (Spiritual Health).

Item 3: TestWell®—National Wellness Institute. https://nationalwellness.org/testwell/index.php?id=1696&id_tier=3430

Item 4: Adams, T., Bezner, J., & Steinhardt, M. (1997). The conceptualization and measurement of perceived wellness: Integrating balance across and within dimensions. *American Journal of Health Promotion*, 11(3), 208–218. https://doi.org/10.4278/0890-1171-11.3.208

Items 5 and 6: Kirk, K. M., Eaves, L .J., & Martin, N. G. (1999). Self-transcendence as a measure of spirituality in a sample of older Australian twins. *Twin Research and Human Genetics*, 2(2), 81–87. https://doi.org/10.1375/twin.2.2.81

Item 7: Levenson, M. R., Jennings, P. A., Aldwin, C. M., & Shiraishi, R. W. (2005). Self-transcendence: Conceptualization and measurement. *The International Journal of Aging and Human Development*, 60(2), 127–143. https://doi.org/10.2190/XRXM-FYRA-7U0X-GRC0

Item 8: from Self-Transcendence Scale, by Reed, P. G. (1986). Developmental resources and depression in the elderly. *Nursing Research*, 35(6), 368–374. https://doi.org/10.1097/00006199-198611000-00014

Item 9: from Self-Transcendence Scale, by Piedmont, R. L. (1999). Does spirituality represent the sixth factor of personality? Spiritual transcendence and the five-factor model. *Journal of Personality*, 67(6), 985–1013. https://doi.org/10.1111/1467-6494.00080

Item 10: DeCicco, T. L., & Stroink, M. L. (2007). A third model of self-construal: The metapersonal self. *International Journal of Transpersonal Studies, 26*(1), 82–104. https://digitalcommons.ciis.edu/ijts-transpersonalstudies/vol26/iss1/9/

Item 11: Diebels, K. J., & Leary, M. R. (2019). The psychological implications of believing that everything is one. *The Journal of Positive Psychology, 14*(4), 463–473. https://doi.org/10.1080/17439760.2018.1484939

For readers who want a deeper dive into this field, here are other key research articles:

Ano, G. G., & Vasconcelles, E. B. (2005). Religious coping and psychological adjustment to stress: A meta-analysis. *Journal of Clinical Psychology, 61*(4), 461–480. https://doi.org/10.1002/jclp.20049

de Jager Meezenbroek, E., Garssen, B., van den Berg, M., van Dierendonck, D., Visser, A., & Schaufeli, W. B. (2012). Measuring spirituality as a universal human experience: A review of spirituality questionnaires. *Journal of Religion and Health, 51*(2), 336–354. https://doi.org/10.1007/s10943-010-9376-1

Haugan, G. (2014). Nurse–patient interaction is a resource for hope, meaning in life and self-transcendence in nursing home patients. *Scandinavian Journal of Caring Sciences, 28*(1), 74–88. https://doi.org/10.1111/scs.12028

Koltko-Rivera, M. E. (2006). Rediscovering the later version of Maslow's hierarchy of needs: Self-transcendence and opportunities for theory, research, and unification. *Review of General Psychology, 10*(4), 302–317. https://doi.org/10.1037/1089-2680.10.4.302

Sawatzky, R., Ratner, P. A., & Chiu, L. (2005). A meta-analysis of the relationship between spirituality and quality of life. *Social Indicators Research, 72*(2), 153–188. https://doi.org/10.1007/s11205-004-5577-x

Schnell, T. (2009). The sources of meaning and meaning in life questionnaire (SoMe): Relations to demographics and well-being. *The Journal of Positive Psychology, 4*(6), 483–499. https://doi.org/10.1080/17439760903271074

(pages 120–121) When Is the Temple? Abraham Joshua Heschel wrote the book *The Sabbath* (1951, Farrar, Straus & Giroux). It contains many wonderful passages that explain the sacredness of time as distinct from space and how this sanctity is expressed in and by the day of rest (Sabbath).

(page 122) The Dungeon in the Temple … the shadow. The concept of shadow pertains to everything about ourselves that we disown, abandon, or deny. Many writers, especially psychologists who follow the work of Carl Jung, claim that we cannot be fully present to our life without embracing the shadow. *QfP Book 5* looks at the shadow side of every Treasure in life. We can encounter the shadow and experience Presence in every moment of this happening life. There is a wealth of information (Johnson, 1994; Zweig & Abrams, 1991) and practices (Bonario et al., n.d.; Brussat & Brussat, 2020) to help us get in touch with the shadow. Access through http://theqeffect.com/ or https://www.theartofquantumliving.com.

Bonario, R., Simmons, G & Simmons, J (n.d.). *The Q effect: The Q process worksheets & workbook for the 21-day practice*. The Quantum Living Process.

Brussat, F., & Brussat, M. A. (2020). *Spiritual practices: Shadow*. Spirituality & Practice: Resources for Spiritual Journeys. https://www.spiritualityandpractice.com/practices/alphabet/view/29/shadow

Johnson, R. A. (1994). *Owning your own shadow: Understanding the dark side of the psyche*. HarperSanFrancisco.

Zweig, C., & Abrams, J. (Eds.). (1991). *Meeting the shadow: The hidden power of the dark side of human nature*. Jeremy P. Tarcher/Penguin.

CHAPTER 10

(pages 125–127) **The metaphor of the veil.** This chapter is a preview of Book 4, which focuses on the eight diverse manifestations of time that we experience day-to-day—on a surface basis—as Routine, Scheduling, Transition, Timing, Rhythm, Transcendence, Interruption, and Pacing. It is the latter manifestation—Transcendence—where the Soulful Capacities intersect with daily life.

Quotation in this chapter from Hazrat Inayat Khan is from https://quotefancy.com/.

CHAPTER 12

(page 142) **Personality, behavior, and the environment.** The thesis that our behavior is a function of the interaction between our personality and the situations we find ourselves in has been well supported in psychological research. However, as much as psychologists try to explain behavior with personality, there is always unexplained variance and many moderating factors (Snyder & Ickes, 1985). Still, the more that "context" and "consistency" is taken into consideration, the more we can explain. In the context of this Book 2, there has been significant growth of research on the role of values and virtues, spiritual intelligence, and "ultimate concerns" (Emmons, 1999) in personality. Book 3 is devoted to a new system of personality that integrates the Radiant Forces (Book 1) and Soulful Capacities (Book 2).

Amram, Y., & Dryer, C. (2008, August 14–17). *The integrated spiritual intelligence scale (ISIS): Development and preliminary validation*. [Paper presentation]. 116th Annual Conference of the American Psychological Association, Boston, MA, United States.

Emmons, R. A. (1999). *The psychology of ultimate concerns: Motivation and spirituality in personality*. The Guilford Press.

King, D. B., & DeCicco, T. L. (2009). A viable model and self-report measure of spiritual intelligence. *International Journal of Transpersonal Studies, 28*(1), 68–85, Article 8. https://doi.org/10.24972/ijts.2009.28.1.68

Mischel, W., & Shoda, Y. (1995). A cognitive-affective system theory of personality: Reconceptualizing situations, dispositions, dynamics, and invariance in personality structure. *Psychological Review, 102*(2), 246–268. https://doi.org/10.1037/0033-295X.102.2.246

Mischel, W., Shoda, Y., & Mendoza-Denton, R. (2002). Situation-behavior profiles as a locus of consistency in personality. *Current Directions in Psychological Science, 11*(2), 50–54. https://doi.org/10.1111/1467-8721.00166

Shaffer, J. A., & Postlethwaite, B. E. (2012). A matter of context: A meta-analytic investigation of the relative validity of contextualized and noncontextualized personality measures. *Personnel Psychology, 65*(3), 445–494. https://doi.org/10.1111/j.1744-6570.2012.01250.x

Shangari, T. R. (2014). *Sant charandas*. Radha Soami Satsang Beas.

Shryack, J., Steger, M. F., Krueger, R. F., & Kallie, C. S. (2010). The structure of virtue: An empirical investigation of the dimensionality of the virtues in action inventory of strengths. *Personality and Individual Differences, 48*(6), 714–719. https://doi.org/10.1016/j.paid.2010.01.007

Snyder, M., & Ickes, W. (1985). Personality and social behavior. In G. Lindzey & E. Aronson (Eds.), *Handbook of Social Psychology* (3rd Edition, pp. 883–947). Random House.

(pages 142–143) Relationship between psyche and cosmos. The application of personality to the Quest for Presence revolves around our capacity or potential to experience the Treasures of life (Book 5). Richard Tarnas discusses the relationship between the human mind and cosmology through the framework of astrology (see https://cosmosandpsyche.com/). Not every reader will accept Tarnas's thesis for astrology as a serious discipline. However, the basic idea resonates with other thinkers: namely, that the human mind (psyche) and the universe (cosmos) have a deep and inextricable relationship to one another, that the cosmos is neither something separate from us, nor does it influence us only from the outside, that the universe is alive with intelligence, and the psyche is representative of and an intimate part of that intelligence. While astrology provides a temporal framework for glimpsing the astonishing coincidences and connections between psyche and cosmos, it is only one temporal framework (see Yiassemides, 2013).

Tarnas, R. (2006). *Cosmos and psyche: Intimations of a new world view*. Viking Books.

Yiassemides, A. (2013). *Time and timelessness: Temporality in the theory of Carl Jung*. Routledge.

Quotation from Hafiz is from Hafiz, & Ladinsky, D. J. (2006). *I heard God laughing: Poems of hope and joy*. Penguin Books.

Quotation in this chapter from Caroline Myss is from https://Goodreads.com.

Acknowledgments

This is the tale of two journeys: My own story and also the story of the Quest for Presence collection itself. Throughout the books in the QfP collection, I acknowledge many teachers, friends, and family for their contribution to my story. For those personal acknowledgements, I direct readers to the books, especially Chapter 7 in Book 3.

But the story of this entire Quest for Presence—the many who helped birth it, and its many phases—all began with several opportunities to share early ideas. Thanks to Dr. Steve Duck, Lawrence Erlbaum Press published *Time and Intimacy: A New Science of Personal Relationships* in 2000. These were research and academic ideas. I yearned to have more practical conversations and started searching. I was first graced with the open arms of the C. G. Jung Society of North Texas (thank you, Maureen Lumley), Unity Church of Dallas and also of Fort Worth, Magellan Healthcare, and also Brandeis University (thank you, Marci McPhee), all of whom brought me in to conduct workshops or retreats in 2000 and early 2001. These offerings had titles like "The Quest for Presence: Time & the Transformation of Work," "Time & Intimacy: Finding Serenity in a Busy World," and "Time and the Soul's Journey." Positive reactions from many participants suggested my ideas had personal relevance.

Around that time, I sent a copy of *Time and Intimacy* to the then-editor of *Spirituality & Health* magazine, Stephen Kiesling. Steve was a key to everything that came next. Through several great conversations, he helped me to reimagine my early drafts of the Quest for Presence Inventory™ (QFPI™). Thanks to Steve for publishing "Navigating in Time" in his magazine in the Winter 2002 issue. I received some calls from readers of that article. One, in particular, was a bookstore owner who encouraged me to write a book.

I also continued to offer workshops, especially at the National Wellness Institute (NWI) in Stevens Point, Wisconsin. I also delivered a train-the-trainer workshop at NWI on "Time and Spiritual Health." Then, the Center for Substance Abuse Prevention (CSAP) at the Substance Abuse and Mental Health Services Administration (SAMHSA) provided further support. Because of a CSAP research grant, between 2002 and 2004 I was able to deliver "Time and Spiritual Health" to employees at small businesses in the Dallas-Fort Worth Metroplex as part of a randomized clinical trial. I especially want to thank Dr. Deborah Galvin, who helped me navigate the grant application and implementation process.

This research study made the concepts even more real. My colleagues (from the Recovery Resource Council in Fort Worth) and I taught "Time and Spiritual Health" to employees in diverse occupations, including car wash attendants, construction workers, engineers, employees in a manufacturing plant, school bus drivers, university administrators, teachers, and physical plant staff. When results from our research with these "everyday" people showed improvements in well-being, I knew these ideas were no longer just academic concepts. Thanks to Richard Sledz, Camille Patterson, Kelly Heath, Wyndy Wiitala and the whole team who helped to implement this study. Thanks to Shawn Reynolds for getting these research findings published.

The many conversations with dozens of these early colleagues and students laid the foundation for the next phase of this work. I am grateful to them and apologize for not mentioning them all. This next phase began with writing. The first draft of Quest for Presence was actually a single book. I asked Sandra Wendel (of Write On, Inc.), the editor for my previous book, Raw Coping Power: From Stress to Thriving, to start editing. Instead, Sandy suggested I first have a group of beta readers provide feedback. She recommended approaching individuals who were familiar with my work as well as others who did not know me.

This five-book Quest for Presence collection emerged as a result of the in-depth, honest, and very insightful feedback from twenty beta readers. Sandy received the feedback anonymously but separately shared the names of reviewers. I am grateful to Sandy for her ongoing guidance (then and now) and to each and every one of the reviewers: Art Wimberly, Briane Agostinelli, Cassie Menn, Cynthia Conigliaro, Gary Loper, Heather Sittler, Heidi Postupack, Janette Helm, Jaymee Spannring, Katharine Hunter, Kimberly Gray, Laura Anne Crowder, Michele Studer, Paul Feather, Rachel Kopke, Regina Novak, Rose Whitcomb, Sadie Liller, Sandy Kogut, and Teresa Przetocki. I also appreciate input from Faith Geiger, Rachael Baker, Janet DeLong and many others who I likely have forgotten. Oh, Wait! Special thanks to Kimberly Gray for always reminding me about the quantum "popping in."

These reviewers were given a list of almost 20 questions, providing a structure for their reactions to the book. Nonetheless, I was overwhelmed with the sheer amount and detail of feedback—almost 20,000 words and over 40 pages. My colleague Shelby Pittman combed through the data searching for common words and themes. Her analysis revealed that readers were excited about the content but overwhelmed by the complexity and depth of the ideas. Importantly, they wanted to retain all the key features of the book; for example, the spiritual message, the odes, the contemplations, and my own story. Many suggested that several books and a separate workbook would make the quest easier to digest. Shelby helped me take the next step to start restructuring the book.

At the same time, I had started teaching virtual courses of "The Quest for Presence." The students who took the class also helped me further refine ideas, and several contributed their QFPI™ profiles (see Book 3). These students included Anissa Amason, Briane Agostinelli, Laura Anne Crowder, Cynthia Conigliaro, Tracey Cox, Madge Cruse, Tyler Currier, Melanie DuPon, Shahinaz Elhennawi, Kristie Ellison, Brenda Fister, Kimberly Gray, Deborah Hamlin, Susan Hansen, Mark Head, Lucy Hoblitzelle, Kathleen Klug, Lindsay Levin, Michele

Mariscal, Jennifer Markley, Jocelyne Maurice, Wesley Miller, Renee Moy, Alan Porzio, Sazha Ramos, Desiree Reynolds, Sandy Salvo, John Shelton, Stephany Sherry, Andy Siegle, John Steakley, Michele Studer, Zac Tolbert, Melanie Weinberger, Art Wimberly, and Susan Yenzer. Thank you for your presence.

Throughout this process, I have been most grateful to those contributing a "treasure story" (see Book 1 and Book 5). This includes a number of people already mentioned, as well as Kathy Carlton, Sara Christopher (Acker), Michaela Conley, and John Weaver. Thank you for reminding me that the treasures are real and true.

Repackaging a single document into multiple volumes and a workbook was daunting. I want to thank Shelby again for her help. Also, Aldrich Chan went through manuscripts, collated all the research references, and found the proper citations for the hundreds of research notes found at the back of every book. Both Shelby's and Aldrich's responsiveness to my requests was a tremendous aid that kept me going.

The final phase of this story was guided by my editors. First, thanks to Sue Hansen of Duck Sauce Life for her exquisite detail in meaningful developmental reviews. Sue's questions, along with her own personal insights, helped me to further clarify ideas in substantive rewrites. Candace Johnson took these edited drafts and, with great thoughtfulness, helped to refine final drafts. Thank you, Sue and Candace, for your patient and thorough work.

Special thanks go to others who helped with design: Gary Rosenberg (from The Book Couple) for beautiful interior design and book covers, Jeffrey McQuirk for his ideas and patience in rendering the images of the four radiant forces, and my dear friend Ellen McCown for her gentle spirit and suggestions for artwork.

At the start of this acknowledgment section, I refer readers to reading the books to find acknowledgments of people in my personal life. I also have to give special thanks to my friends Art Wimberly, Spencer Seidman, and Cynthia Conigliaro—each of whom spent many hours listening to me ramble on and on about my struggles as a writer on this quest of time. Their playful feedback helped me feel so much less alone during periods of dismay and doubt. Thanks, guys!

Finally, I could say that none of this would have been possible without the love, support, and kindest patience of my wife, Jan. The truth is, I could have pulled off some of it … maybe. However, I know it would not be anything approaching the rich tapestry that I hope readers see through so many words. My own ability to see this tapestry—of the preciousness of this life and my love of life—comes from Jan. She, more than anyone I have ever known, lightens me, gives me confidence, and so makes it possible for me to listen more and listen deeply. I am so grateful for her and our many years together.

About the Author

Joel Bennett, PhD, is president of Organizational Wellness & Learning Systems (OWLS), a consulting firm that specializes in evidence-based wellness and e-learning technologies to promote organizational health and employee well-being. Dr. Bennett first delivered stress management programming in 1985, and through the efforts of over 400 resilience facilitators and coaches who have been trained in OWLS' evidence-informed curriculum as well as consulting in South Africa, Italy, and Brazil, OWLS programs have since reached over 250,000 workers across the United States and internationally. OWLS has received over $6 million in National Institutes of Health funding for workplace well-being research, and their programs have been recognized as effective by independent bodies, including the US Surgeon General.

OWLS consults on Integral Organizational Wellness™ approaches that combine leadership, champion, team, and peer-to-peer strategies: nudging the true culture of health. Joel is the author of 50 peer-reviewed research articles and chapters and has authored or coauthored eight books, including *Heart-Centered Leadership* (with Susan Steinbrecher), *Raw Coping Power: From Stress to Thriving, Your Best Self at Work* (with Ben Dilla), *Well-Being Champions: A Competency-Based Guidebook, Time and Intimacy, Preventing Workplace Substance Abuse*, and *The Connoisseur of Time.*

Dr. Bennett has served in advisory and board roles for various organizations including Magellan Health; Aetna; the National Wellness Institute; It's Time Texas, Work Healthier Advisory Committee; the Academy of Management Division on Management and

Spirituality; the Global Wellness Institute; the International Foundation of Employee Benefits Plans; and the State of Texas Primary Prevention Planning Committee (Preventing Sexual Violence).

In 2022, he received the William B. Baun Lifetime Achievement Award from the National Wellness Institute for his contributions to the professional field of wellness. He also received the Positive Leadership Award from the Positive Leadership Institute for forward-thinking management practices that help employees, teams, and organizations thrive.

Joel lives in North Texas with Jan, his wife of twenty-eight years, and around the corner from his wonderful son, daughter-in-law, and grandchildren, who call him "Obi." He hopes that one day he will become a Jedi Knight or something.